Power Play:
Empowerment of the African American Student-Athlete

Power Play: Empowerment of the African American Student-Athlete

Enzley Mitchell IV, Ph.D.

Library of Congress Control Number:		2018909317
ISBN:	Hardcover	978-1-9845-4559-6
	Softcover	978-1-9845-4558-9
	eBook	978-1-9845-4557-2

Print information available on the last page.

Rev. date: 12/03/2020

To order additional copies of this book, contact:
Xlibris
844-714-8691
www.Xlibris.com
Orders@Xlibris.com
783233

CONTENTS

To my two biggest supporters and my biggest critics: Mom and Dad. I have shared all of my successes with both of you, and you have been there for many of them. You both always took time to listen to all of my ideas and dreams. I could always depend on Dad to grill me, ask me the tough questions, and make sure what I was thinking was well thought out. Thank you for all of your support over the years and believing in me. I love you Mom and Dad.

To my inspiration and the one I do everything for: the people I love more than anyone in this world—my beautiful daughter Kenley and wife Kendra—the reasons I push myself everyday in everything I do and the reasons I have not given up. Both of you have made me a better person and always strive to be the best Dad and husband ever.

ABOUT THE AUTHOR

ENZLEY MITCHELL IV, Ph.D. is the founder of PrepSearch LLC. where he serves as CEO and is an independent Educational Consultant. Dr. Mitchell provides college success education in high schools to prospective student-athletes, guidance counselors and parents. He also assists families with the college athletics recruiting process. PrepSearch was created in 2007 and has helped hundreds of prospective student-athletes choose the right college or university for them. PrepSearch offers a free database and search engine for prospective student-athletes and their families at www.prepsearch.net. When Dr. Mitchell is not providing college success education, he serves as an Assistant Professor of Sport Management and Head Men's Basketball Coach at Saint Mary of the Woods College.

Mitchell has college coaching and administrative experience at the NAIA, NCAA Division I, and NCAA Division III levels, serving as director of athletics or a head basketball coach. Positions in intercollegiate athletics include assistant men's basketball coach at Earlham College, Assistant Men's basketball coach at Wilberforce University, director of basketball operations at IUPUI, assistant women's basketball coach at IUPUI, assistant men's basketball coach at Millikin University, head men's basketball coach at Northern New Mexico College, and head men's basketball coach at Illinois Institute of Technology. In addition to his coaching experience, Mitchell has served as director of athletics at Northern New Mexico College, Illinois Institute of Technology, and Harris Stowe State University.

Mitchell was born and raised in Fort Wayne, Indiana and is a graduate of Snider High School where he played varsity basketball. After graduating from Snider High School, he attended Spring Arbor University where he played basketball and was a 4-year varsity athlete. At Spring Arbor, Mitchell helped lead his team to a conference co-championship, earned first team all -conference, first team all defense, and defensive player of the year honors before graduating with a bachelor's degree in Business Administration. Following graduation, he played professional basketball in Europe including one season as head coach of the Swansea Basketball club in Swansea Wales, leading the team to a 19-4 record and semi-final appearance in the premier league championship.

In addition to earning a bachelor's degree while a student-athlete, Mitchell also earned a Master's degree in Recreation & Sport Management from Indiana State University and a Ph.D. in Sport Administration from Concordia University Chicago.

Living in the Indianapolis area, Mitchell enjoys spending time with his wife, daughter, and Miniature Pinscher named Kobe. An avid sports fan, he enjoys watching college football, college basketball, the NBA, NFL, and NASCAR racing.

ACKNOWLEDGEMENTS

THERE ARE SO many people I need to thank for their assistance, inspiration, and encouragement to write this book. At the same time, there are many people who helped me to write this book and did not realize it. I first want to praise and thank God for blessing my family and I during this endeavor. My wife Kendra would not let me forget about the idea I had over a decade before starting this. I can even remember the number of times we discussed the topic in general as well as my specific recommendations for reform and change needed to get African American student-athletes off of the plantation.

A big thanks to my dissertation chair at Concordia University, Dr. Pamela Konkol: she was a tremendous help to me in getting my ideas formulated correctly and in a way that would adequately get my point across. During the times we discussed the idea for my book while working on my dissertation, Dr. Konkol constantly reminded me how important he topic was and how I was the person who needed to deliver the message.

A special thanks to Jerry Berardi: without your help, I would not have completed my dissertation or this book.

Thank you to two of my assistant basketball coaches who listened and encouraged me on many of our long road trips and post-game meals. I cannot thank them enough for their honest feedback as well as sharing an equal passion for the topic.

Then there are the former student-athletes I have met along the way in my journey as a coach and athletics administrator. Too many of them to mention, but each with a familiar story about the system, the coaches, the institutions, the association, and the feeling of being used and exploited when their playing days were over.

One former student-athlete that I had the pleasure of talking to at length, I will call him "Jayden." I appreciated getting to know Jayden and really putting a face on the aftermath of what happens to many

African American student-athletes who play in a revenue sport at the Division I level. Sharing about being told to take the minimum hours needed to remain eligible, participating in the NCAA men's Division I basketball tournament, and completing his eligibility but not completing the requirements to earn his degree. This same former Division I African American student-athlete talked about how nearly five years after playing in his last college game he still has no degree, and the coaching staff at the university was immediately different once he could no longer play for the institution.

I want to thank many of my friends and colleagues—some who knew they were directly contributing to this book and others who contributed timely input and encouragement. I appreciate all of the conversations with each of you whether it was about basketball, life, career, or this book: friends, former coaches, former players, former teammates, and colleagues.

There is one last person I'd like to thank for reading this book whether you agree with me, whether you don't or are somewhere in between. I hope my message and proposals encourage you to speak, write, email, talk, or march about whatever issue in life you feel called to and start to make a difference.

INTRODUCTION

WRITING A BOOK about empowering African American student-athletes has been on my mind for quite awhile. I first began thinking about this topic when I was a college basketball coach and even more, once I became a college athletic director. I write this book not as a scholar but as a disgruntled fan of college basketball and football, a former African American student-athlete, a former college basketball coach, and a former college athletic director (AD).

This book is not intended to be a race-baiting commentary on the state of intercollegiate athletics or whether to pay all student-athletes. As I state many times throughout this book, my main concern is seeing fair distribution of revenue for student-athletes in revenue sports. This cannot occur without stopping the exploitation of the African American students that comprise the majority of basketball and football rosters and making suggestions for a system that sets these and all student-athletes up for academic success and leaving their institution prepared to start whatever career they may choose.

This book is not intended to be a place where I complain about what I personally perceive is lack of leadership at the top of the NCAA. I will leave that for others. I do place much of the blame squarely on those in positions of power and influence at the Power Five institutions, including presidents, ADs, and head coaches. People in these positions are standing in the way of any type of reform because of serving their own personal interests and those of their institutions. The topic of paying student-athletes, revenue sports, and the influence of African American student-athletes is a very sensitive subject that sadly runs along racial lines.

One study that confirms the racial division of this topic was published in the Political Research Quarterly and written by Kevin Wallsten, Tatishe Mteta, Lauren McCarthy, and Melinda Tarsi. The study conducted in 2014 titled *Prejudice or Principled Conservatism?*

Racial Resentment and White Opinion toward Paying College Athletes came to several conclusions. These included:

- Whites are more likely than Blacks to oppose college athlete pay-for-play.
- Harboring negative racial views about Blacks is the single strongest predictor of White opposition to paying athletes—more important than age, education level, political affiliation, sports fandom, or even if Whites had participated in college sports themselves.
- The more negatively Whites feel about Blacks, the more they oppose pay-for-play.
- Racially resentful Whites who are primed to think about African-American athletes before answering questions are more likely to oppose paying athletes than racially resentful Whites who are primed to think about White athletes.

I fully support fair distribution of revenue in Division I football, men's, and women's basketball. I am also a staunch advocate of the African American student-athlete in all sports. Just as I want to see all students succeed academically, compete for whatever higher education institution they chose, and graduate with a degree in the area they are interested in, I do not want to see *any* student taken advantage of, treated inequitably, or exploited.

That being said, I have watched the continued commercialization of Division I athletics and feel as many others do that it has clearly led to the exploitation of a segment of student-athletes that are majority African American. As I sit in my home office watching the beginning of another NCAA Division I men's basketball tournament, I am disappointed. I am disappointed that I have over a decade of notes for this book and still have not written anything. I am disappointed that more people like myself have not spoken up and taken any action on the exploitation of some of the student-athletes in this tournament. I am disappointed that while my notes have gathered dust, no meaningful reform has occurred to create a better system to help the student-athletes receive a small portion of the millions of dollars in revenue they are directly responsible for generating. I'm disappointed that some of the talented young men I'm watching today will not graduate while the organization just runs another commercial touting where students athletes are going after graduation.

The issue for me runs much deeper than simple exploitation of African American student-athletes in the Division I revenue sports. There are multiple double standards at play here. Coaches can leave without fulfilling their contract, but students cannot transfer without sitting out a year. The organization claims its governance is for the benefit of the student-athlete, yet most of their rules are aimed at punishing students. There are limitations on employment and so-called "extra benefits." Accept something as small as a lunch, a haircut, or ride to the airport, and a student-athlete can put their eligibility at risk.

I will get into my thoughts on the benefits I think student-athletes should receive later in this book.

As you read this book, you will see that I am very passionate about this topic as are many of you. Empowering the African American student-athlete is one way to promote change in intercollegiate athletics for all student-athletes and create a fair distribution of the revenue that these students help to generate. I am in support of rewarding *all* student-athletes—regardless of their sport—something beyond their athletic aid and cost of attendance. I completely understand that some institutions can afford this and others cannot. I also understand the implications (positive) this could have for Title IX and the future of some men's sports (negative). Nonetheless, there may not be a completely fair way to address this situation, but then again, life is not fair either. Fair or not, if you do not help generate the revenue, you do not have any say in this debate. Non-revenue sports equal no power, at least in the Power Five (Atlantic Coast Conference, Big 12 Conference, Big Ten Conference, Pac-12 Conference, and Southeastern Conference) world. Harsh, but true, only because in many of those institutions the "non" revenue sports exist as a direct result of the efforts and labor of exploited students in football and men's basketball.

For this book, I give my opinion based on elite student-athletes in the revenue sports of football, men's basketball, and women's basketball at the NCAA Division I level. I am defining an elite student-athlete as one who plays in the sports of football, men's basketball, or women's basketball who could potentially be drafted into the NFL, NBA, or WNBA. These student-athletes also have the potential to continue their careers professionally in many other leagues such as the NBA G-League, Canadian Football League, Arena Football League, Alliance of American Football (AAF), Xtreme Football League (XFL), or any of the dozens of professional basketball leagues for men and women outside of the United States. I am in no way saying that elite athletes are found in only these sports. It is simply for the sake of this book where I am limiting the discussion.

I fully understand there are many other student-athletes (including African Americans) who compete in sports such as baseball, ice hockey, soccer, tennis, golf, swimming, and diving, and track & field that will have an opportunity to have lucrative professional careers. I am only interested in the college sports that generate the largest amount of revenue for the NCAA Power Five conference members and have the largest numbers of African American students on their rosters.

I feel that some significant and meaningful reform is needed in intercollegiate athletics, more specifically, in NCAA Division I. Waiting for college presidents, AD's, and coaches to make change will not work. It is simply not in the best interest of these stakeholder groups to push for change. Why would they? Student-athlete welfare certainly has not truly been a priority for many college presidents, AD's, and coaches up to this point. There is too much for members of each of these groups to lose.

This brings me to the title of this book and trying to identify what changes the African American student-athlete can directly affect. You might ask why am I singling out this group of students. I choose this group of students in football, and men's and women's basketball because these are the three sports in the Power Five conferences that have the greatest chance of generating revenue for the institution, and also have a disproportionate number of African American student-athletes on their rosters. As I read a quote from Big 12 commissioner Bob Bowlsby, it reminded me of something I want to make very clear in this book: I am in no way saying students in non-revenue sports, student-athletes in sports that operate at a loss, student-athletes who compete in sports with little or no African American representation on their rosters or coaching staff in anyway way are less committed, don't work as hard, and are not entitled to the best athletics experience their institution can provide for all student-athletes. I thought Bowlsby's quote was interesting and telling coming from a Power Five conference commissioner. He said:

> It is hard to justify paying student-athletes in football and men's basketball and not recognizing the significant effort that swimmers and wrestlers and lacrosse players and track athletes all put in. Football and basketball players don't work any harder than anybody else; they just happen to have the blessing of an adoring public who is willing to pay for the tickets and willing to buy the products on television that come with the high visibility. (Trahan, 2014)

As part of the adoring public, I just happen to be a huge fan of college football and college basketball: that is my choice and my right. I also understand that at many institutions several of the sports teams like swimming, wrestling, or track, exist in part because of allocations from student fees and subsidies from their football and basketball programs. It does not minimize any other sports importance or the effort the student-athletes who participate in those sports put in. I do not like seeing any student-athlete treated unfairly or student-athletes not being adequately rewarded for their talents. I would still feel this way if we were talking about swimming, wrestling, lacrosse, track, or any other college sport.

The issues in this book are driven by the interest in a few particularly popular college sports. It is particularly sensitive for many people because there is a racial component involved. In addition to talking about what I feel is the exploitation of African American student-athletes, I also make two proposals for reform, which I will discuss later in this book, that involve distribution of athletics revenue, increasing graduation rates, and setting up *all* student-athletes for success well after their eligibility has been exhausted. When I was a college AD, I used to tell my coaches and staff that they could not complain about something and not offer a solution.

Facts and Figures

A 2013 study by the University of Pennsylvania's Center for the Study of Race and Equity in Education found that 57% of football players and 64% of men's basketball players in the six largest Division I conferences are African-American; at the same schools, African-American men made up less than 3% of the overall student population (Harper, Wiliams, & Blackman, 2013). In recent NFL drafts, five times as many African American players have been taken in the first two rounds. AD's and coaches, meanwhile, are overwhelmingly White (Yee, 2016). I also want you to keep this data in mind as you move through the book:

> The demographics of head football and basketball coaches are similar. At the start of the 2014 college football season, 87.5% of head football coaches in the Football Bowl Subdivision were White. In the 2013-14 season, 76% of head basketball coaches in Division I were White. The money generated by football and men's basketball also goes to subsidize "non-revenue" sports such as soccer, equestrian, field hockey, rowing, swimming, gymnastics, and golf. Virtually all of those programs lose money, and most of the men and women playing those sports are White. But at least the subsidies are allowing other athletes to compete at a high level, not funding lavish salaries for executives. (Yee, 2016, para. 24)

Why is such a flawed business model that depends on unpaid labor—mostly by African American student-athletes playing Division I football, men's basketball, and women's basketball—lining the pockets of mostly White administrators and coaches still accepted year after year? I believe it is due to all student-athletes who participate in Division I football, men's basketball, and women's basketball who have not realized their collective economic influence. Those who can help them make changes have no personal reason to do so. There is just too much at stake for university presidents, AD's, and coaches at the student-athletes expense. Before I get into some recommendations, I want to provide you with the most significant piece of data that provides the start of my discussion.

In addition to helping to promote fair revenue distribution and a change in the present system in Division I sports, student-athletes can also help to move improvements in other areas as well. Student-athletes can use their collective influence to help create more diverse applicant pools as well as training/education for minorities, women, and underrepresented groups. They could help promote needed change in the hiring practices for coaches and administrators by promoting diversity and fairness in hiring searches while still hiring the best person for the job.

The following is a chart listing the revenues of the top 65 NCAA Division I member institutions based on 2015-2016 data submitted to the Department of Education Office of Post Secondary Education and compiled by *USA Today*. The majority of the list is comprised of public Power Five institutions. The information comes from detailed financial disclosure forms that institutions annually submit to the NCAA. The data in the chart is for the fiscal year ending 2016 and available per state and federal public records laws. Ticket revenue is a portion of the pie that is often missed in the discussion of exploitation and whether to pay student-athletes.

University	Ticket Sales	Contributions	Rights/ Licensing
Texas A&M	$47,784,673	$75,457,474	$57,856,867
Texas	$60,870,893	$42,159,118	$75,014,854
Ohio State	$61,362,320	$33,138,103	$60,429,212
Alabama	$40,118,302	$29,651,491	$66,253,910
Michigan	$49,617,039	$37,581,954	$62,697,349
Oklahoma	$39,747,466	$46,641,355	$55,074,491
LSU	$45,222,768	$33,539,802	$57,059,301
Florida	$27,713,183	$43,146,263	$62,151,216
Tennessee	$36,844,478	$34,082,765	$61,453,383
Auburn	$32,165,386	$35,720,710	$54,378,734
Wisconsin	$30,959,974	$21,499,693	$59,086,137
Penn State	$35,188,377	$26,183,278	$53,139,471
Kentucky	$37,195,389	$25,039,404	$65,400,012
Arkansas	$37,424,186	$25,860,510	$58,473,384
Georgia	$28,024,404	$33,301,406	$56,179,285
Michigan State	$24,684,212	$30,441,924	$53,914,039
South Carolina	$25,236,246	$30,346,425	$47,696,767
Florida State	$20,206,022	$32,382,845	$36,140,389
Minnesota	$23,889,905	$15,250,676	$51,849,920
Iowa	$25,667,416	$27,799,738	$48,862,045
Louisville	$29,054,868	$30,391,706	$38,148,302
Nebraska	$37,198,005	$21,518,119	$48,303,151
Oregon	$25,745,016	$28,036,119	$44,778,495
Mississippi	$20,616,537	$31,692,460	$50,160,473
Washington	$25,381,191	$23,186,969	$48,687,243
West Virginia	$19,354,989	$33,485,350	$44,253,779
Clemson	$23,537,134	$35,639,063	$33,738,363
Virginia	$14,612,987	$31,556,907	$39,626,803
UCLA	$18,361,978	$15,493,926	$48,536,337
Missouri	$19,152,889	$19,982,560	$48,545,576

Student Fees	School Funds	Other	Total Revenues
$0	$0	$13,289,436	$194,388,450
$0	$0	$9,936,293	$187,981,158
$0	$77,139	$15,782,991	$170,789,765
$0	$7,991,579	$19,994,463	$164,009,745
$0	$266,467	$13,687,807	$163,850,616
$0	$0	$8,909,904	$150,373,216
$0	$0	$5,829,589	$141,651,460
$2,431,579	$1,998,856	$4,000,012	$141,441,109
$1,000,000	$0	$7,068,329	$140,448,955
$5,000,051	$1,955,376	$10,850,336	$140,070,593
$0	$8,351,045	$12,891,877	$132,788,726
$0	$0	$17,736,950	$132,248,076
$912,981	$0	$3,632,460	$132,180,246
$0	$2,335,332	$887,630	$124,981,042
$3,233,143	$0	$3,103,030	$123,841,268
$0	$1,433,603	$12,560,717	$123,034,495
$0	$3,229,616	$15,822,038	$122,331,092
$8,364,645	$0	$16,660,413	$113,754,314
$0	$7,055,984	$15,459,794	$113,506,279
$650,000	$0	$10,269,821	$113,249,020
$1,987,361	$5,415,733	$7,148,534	$112,146,504
$0	$0	$5,123,686	$112,142,961
$1,766,553	$453,200	$10,921,792	$111,701,175
$1,911,778	$2,577,501	$3,565,956	$110,524,705
$0	$1,986,414	$7,912,743	$107,154,560
$3,992,498	$47,298	$4,006,454	$105,140,368
$0	$4,634,488	$7,274,009	$104,823,057
$13,730,496	$0	$3,745,126	$103,272,319
$2,598,559	$60,000	$13,862,223	$98,913,023
$0	$1,015,000	$8,579,814	$97,275,839

University	Ticket Sales	Contributions	Rights/ Licensing
Illinois	$14,604,625	$28,531,388	$44,433,775
Indiana	$17,388,154	$20,467,570	$49,690,229
North Carolina	$23,332,957	$22,926,465	$33,669,653
Mississippi State	$16,024,676	$23,136,962	$52,583,747
Arizona State	$11,899,256	$16,660,713	$43,990,484
Maryland	$16,493,833	$13,676,004	$46,175,076
Oklahoma State	$22,019,465	$17,931,099	$40,293,984
Kansas	$19,400,723	$24,020,732	$44,238,082
Arizona	$15,433,644	$18,904,155	$38,271,043
Rutgers	$13,757,852	$8,980,761	$20,070,475
Virginia Tech	$18,053,062	$19,348,259	$32,590,246
Texas Tech	$10,999,848	$24,147,562	$38,493,352
California	$10,690,053	$19,774,870	$37,185,376
NC State	$19,017,232	$15,119,174	$37,032,338
Utah	$16,976,245	$8,549,247	$38,399,704
Connecticut	$10,362,040	$6,166,461	$24,587,464
Purdue	$9,972,989	$19,000,750	$45,526,147
Iowa State	$15,626,121	$14,837,823	$41,438,418
Kansas State	$15,493,405	$18,087,939	$40,945,574
Colorado	$12,367,082	$11,018,604	$35,882,482
Georgia Tech	$13,101,709	$11,022,030	$31,593,887
Oregon State	$10,469,199	$8,805,109	$38,485,539
Central Florida	$3,934,495	$6,918,969	$9,063,153
Cincinnati	$7,781,571	$4,662,582	$16,639,872
Washington State	$5,532,126	$7,718,902	$35,207,583
San Diego State	$5,850,716	$10,388,209	$10,749,583
Houston	$4,868,522	$8,143,810	$7,763,475
Memphis	$10,036,174	$10,499,478	$8,241,047
James Madison	$2,783,548	$2,583,519	$3,298,950
South Florida	$3,036,967	$2,942,660	$15,435,038

Student Fees	School Funds	Other	Total Revenues
$3,208,815	$536,456	$4,934,441	$96,249,500
$0	$2,168,073	$5,502,736	$95,216,762
$7,302,963	$1,848,014	$6,095,933	$95,175,985
$0	$0	$3,158,020	$94,903,405
$10,576,696	$9,917,840	$1,617,754	$94,662,743
$11,630,126	$3,789,312	$2,337,346	$94,101,697
$3,707,453	$4,844,208	$4,876,467	$93,672,676
$319,852	$1,489,711	$1,189,729	$90,658,829
$0	$9,537,705	$3,209,689	$85,356,236
$11,421,897	$17,188,776	$12,554,398	$83,974,159
$8,642,256	$2,351	$5,066,524	$83,702,698
$3,282,974	$2,531,257	$3,541,328	$82,996,321
$444,374	$4,555,626	$9,002,725	$81,653,024
$6,603,275	$2,024	$2,450,986	$80,225,029
$6,084,769	$5,835,686	$3,601,861	$79,447,512
$8,280,611	$26,990,210	$2,842,489	$79,229,275
$0	$0	$4,200,090	$78,699,976
$2,111,137	$0	$4,342,001	$78,355,500
$500,695	$0	$2,909,051	$77,936,664
$1,593,693	$11,270,355	$5,144,673	$77,276,889
$5,270,384	$2,171,535	$13,249,748	$76,409,293
$2,597,200	$4,650,200	$7,724,000	$72,731,247
$22,447,191	$4,391,175	$12,624,470	$59,379,453
$0	$24,892,123	$5,086,008	$59,062,156
$818,961	$4,130,892	$5,344,802	$58,753,266
$10,635,088	$15,647,711	$3,279,721	$56,551,028
$7,546,458	$17,609,027	$5,538,005	$51,469,297
$7,387,557	$10,976,828	$2,886,257	$50,027,341
$36,279,395	$1,844,021	$653,215	$47,442,648
$17,032,220	$6,370,829	$2,343,105	$47,160,819

University	Ticket Sales	Contributions	Rights/ Licensing
UNLV	$5,789,602	$8,970,585	$9,978,618
Boise State	$7,853,132	$10,311,076	$12,012,243
Fresno State	$5,368,827	$9,155,151	$8,839,968
Old Dominion	$4,237,654	$5,851,095	$5,155,793
East Carolina	$6,918,040	$9,097,450	$7,499,729
Army	$5,566,875	$5,327,292	$12,323,659

Student Fees	School Funds	Other	Total Revenues
$2,958,156	$15,617,025	$3,572,038	$46,886,024
$3,341,671	$9,316,804	$3,776,842	$46,611,768
$4,472,917	$15,396,665	$1,570,619	$44,804,147
$28,745,710	$0	$691,683	$44,681,935
$14,249,768	$4,647,262	$2,200,835	$44,613,084
$514,020	$13,147,558	$7,311,634	$44,191,038

Credits: Steve Berkowitz, Christopher Schnaars and Mark Hannan of *USA Today*; Mark Alewine, Jennifer Brugh, Rebecca Harris, Jessica Hunt, Cynthia Maldonado Perez, Luis Ulloa Rodriguez, Zhancheng Wu and Kellon Thomas of the Indiana University-Purdue University Indianapolis' Sports Capital Journalism Program.

IMPORTANT DEFINITIONS

Ticket Sales: Gross revenue from ticket sales for all home athletics events.

Contributions: Outside contributions and donations to the institutions athletics department.

Right/Licensing: Income from TV, Radio, Internet, sales of branded merchandise, Sponsorships and Advertising.

Student Fees: Optional or required student fee depending on the institution used to subsidize athletics operations. These fees may range from a few hundred to several thousand dollars per academic year per full time and part time undergraduate student. In many cases online and graduate students do not pay these fees.

School Funds: Subsidy provided from institutional funds

Other: Any amounts included in the total operating revenue that does not fall into one of the categories above and could include: In-kind facility gifts, Conference revenue distribution, and guarantees or money earned by playing at another institution.

Total Revenues: Total operating revenues

CHAPTER 1

Exploited not Empowered

SEVERAL AUTHORS AND scholars who have written on the subject of the unfair treatment of student-athletes have compared the situation to slavery. They even have gone as far as calling the students *slaves* because of their treatment by individual institutions and the association. I cannot disrespect my ancestors and go as far as calling student-athletes slaves. These students have made a choice to provide free labor and give up various freedoms to the institutions they attend. My ancestors did not have a choice in being enslaved, forced into providing free labor, being threatened with violence, raped, murdered, and having their freedom taken. While there are certainly some aspects of slavery present in the treatment of today's student-athletes, ultimately, each makes a choice and chooses the "massa" they serve.

I prefer and will call many of the student-athletes in football, and men's and women's basketball *exploited*, and this exploitation is not limited to just African American students.

I am choosing to use the term exploited to describe the students I am writing about in this book. When you look at the definition of the word *exploit* and the treatment of some student-athletes, primarily those in the revenue sports, applying the term makes sense. I say this because so many want to argue that the current level of athletic aid received by those who get full cost of attendance (tuition, room, board, fees) and a stipend above this say that's enough compensation for these student no matter how much revenue they help generate. I would agree with this if the value that student-athletes provide to their respective institutions was limited to advancing the mission of the institution, helping to drive applications and enrollment through visibility in bowl games and the NCAA basketball tournament, building institutional pride, and enhancing retention efforts; however, such is not the case. The influence is so much greater.

Let me talk specifically about the definition of exploit by giving you some words and phrases that define it: *to take advantage of, impose on, treat unfairly, benefit from, using a person in an unfair or selfish way, to utilize for profit, to advance a cause,* and *to use something in a way that benefits you.* I think we all get the point here. Using slavery as a term is simply not accurate and lazy. There is no violence or loss of life directed towards any student-athlete, so exploited fits perfectly.

For the sake of our discussion, let us figure the total cost of an education at a Power Five university is $50,000 per year. So, for 4 years we are talking about a $200,000 or more investment in a student-athlete who is receiving athletic aid that covers the total cost of attendance over their 4 years of eligibility. I mention this because I want you to keep these hypothetical figures in mind as you move through the chapters in this book and get to proposal 1 and proposal 2 at the end of the book.

Based on the labor these student-athletes are providing and the missed opportunities they have compared to other fulltime non-student-athletes, I want you to consider each of the ways these students are potentially being disadvantaged. I know there are many of you who will say that the $50,000 per year investment that a Power Five university has made in each student-athlete is all they should get, but I challenge you to take a moment with me and just consider some of the numerous ways these students help generate revenue for their institutions and why it is not fair to limit their benefit to the cost of attendance they receive.

The argument that it is the student-athlete's job doesn't work because you and I were hired by our employers and signed an agreement or contract to work for a specific salary with possibly an added commission or bonus. Student-athletes are not employees; they are students who did not sign an *employment* contract. The NCAA actually wants to place limits on the employment student-athletes can have.

Sticking with the argument that student-athletes are compensated by their "full ride" scholarship, the "full ride" is a myth. Only in a best-case scenario are all students in revenue sports at a particular institution receiving athletics aid that covers their cost of attendance 100%.

To set the stage, I'll list several ways Division I student-athletes in revenue sports are exploited, treated unfairly, or taken advantage of in no particular order of importance.

- **Student-athletes will help others earn exorbitant compensation with little direct benefit**. Many coaches, AD's, and conference commissioners, in addition to six and seven figure salaries, are compensated with lucrative bonuses based on individual team performance, student-athlete GPA, and other criteria. The students that help achieve these successes see nothing. Many Power Five commissioners are compensated in excess of $1 million annually. The current president of the NCAA, Mark Emmert, earns $1.7 million based on numbers from a 2011 tax return published in *USA Today*. That number as of 2018 could be substantially higher (Berkowitz, 2013).

- **Student-athletes in revenue sports provide the labor and generate the majority of money that supports the entire system**. The NCAA generates revenue primarily from two sources, and this helps pay for the majority of NCAA operations. According to 2016-2017 unaudited figures from NCAA, the Division I Men's Basketball Championship television and marketing rights generated $821.4 million. Another $129.4 million came from championship ticket sales. Although the majority of this revenue is generated by student-athletes in football and men's basketball, $210.8 million is distributed to Division I member institutions to help fund NCAA sports and to provide scholarships for college athletes and $96.7 million is used to provide college athletes a chance to compete for championships in all sports including support for lodging, team travel, and food (NCAA, n.d.). This is important because the efforts of a few sports with rosters comprised mostly of African American student-athletes support the operations and provide assistance to all sports. A disproportionate number of African

American students competing in football and basketball help generate revenue for sports that often operate at a loss and have little if no African American representation on their rosters or coaching staffs.

- **Transferring from an institution is difficult.** Transfer rules penalize students when they want to change schools but allow coaches to break contracts and leave schools whenever they choose with little or no penalty. In most cases, if a student-athlete wants to transfer from a Division I institution to another Division I institution they will most likely face heavy restrictions on where they can transfer in addition to sitting out a year of competition.

- **Lost income opportunities.** Student-athletes cannot benefit financially from use of their name, image, or likeness. NCAA rules as of 2018 prohibit student-athletes from being able to sell their autographs, sign, and receive paid endorsement contracts of brand apparel and other merchandise as well as various activities where a student-athlete could receive compensation.

- **Missed employment opportunities.** The NCAA places restrictions on the type of employment a student-athlete can have, and the student-athlete has much less time to earn additional income from part-time or summer employment if they need it. There is only limited time to work a part-time job during and out of season, and there are restrictions on income that can be earned. The non-student-athlete does not have to worry about these restrictions.

- **Athletic aid and scholarships are not guaranteed**. A student-athlete is not guaranteed to have his scholarship renewed and may lose it if injured and cannot compete. Many scholarships are annually renewed at the discretion of the coach, although some institutions have moved to offering a guarantee. If possible, a student should get an offer of a guarantee not from athletics but an Admissions Financial Contract Agreement.

- **Student-athletes are subject to abuse and stress more often than non-student-athletes.** Emotional and physical abuse from coaches is not uncommon. For those who say a sport is a student's job and the scholarship is their compensation, the hostile workplace some of these students face is hardly worth it. On top of some of the recent high profile cases of student-athlete emotional, psychological, and physical abuse is the stress that a large number of student-athletes will face. Hinkle (2014, Para. 4) said, "Ten percent of college athletes suffer from psychological and physiological problems that are severe enough to require counseling intervention." However, college student-athletes tend to avoid seeking out available counseling, so the percentage of student-athletes who may actually require such intervention is possibly higher than this figure (Murray, 1997).

- **Many times an athlete must compete sick or injured**. There is no insurance or workmen's compensation to cover student-athletes if they have a career-ending injury to help them finish paying for their education or provide compensation for those determined to have had a professional athletic career in the future. Insurance polices to cover potential loss of earnings in the event of a catastrophic or career-ending injury are available on the student-athlete's own dime.

- **The clothing, shoes, and equipment are a small amount of compensation for student-athletes compared to what many football and basketball coaches will receive.** Coaches often sign apparel and shoe contracts valued upwards of $1,000,000 or more that compensate them in addition to their coaching salary. In exchange for this compensation, the student-athlete is provided with only a nominal amount of apparel and shoes from the manufacturer.

- **The current system does not compensate any student-athlete in any sport for revenue the institution receives from TV, radio, Internet, or pay-per-view broadcasting contracts.** Conference sports networks such as the Big Ten Network generate revenue by broadcasting college sports and selling advertising during the broadcasts. It is unclear how much of this money if any of this goes directly back to the student-athletes competing for the institutions.

- **Student-athletes in revenue sports are highly susceptible to clustering and being victims of academic fraud**. There is a higher probability that a student-athlete may be involved in academic fraud, may be "clustered" into a major they have no interest in and which doesn't meet their career objective, or they are herded into a sham major altogether. There have been numerous cases of academic fraud in recent years. Based on a 2015 analysis by *Inside Higher Ed* of the NCAA's major infraction database, it was found that the NCAA had punished institutions at least 15 times for academic fraud over the last decade. Some of the institutions punished for misconduct have included The University of North Carolina at Chapel Hill, Syracuse, Southern Methodist University, Weber State University, and Georgia Southern University (Inside Higher Education, 2015).

- **Missed endorsement opportunities**. Student-athletes under current rules cannot take advantage of any marketing or endorsement opportunities they may have.

- **Successful teams help generate an increase in college applications and net tuition revenue**. Teams that play in bowl games and have success in the NCAA men's basketball tournament help generate more applications, more enrollments, and ultimately more net tuition revenue for their institutions. In *The Dynamic Advertising Effect of Collegiate Athletics*, a study conducted by Douglas J. Chung of the Harvard Business School, he called this the "Flutie Effect." Just to emphasize the importance of this effect and why student-athletes are missing out, take a look at some of Chung's findings:

  a) When a school rises from mediocre to great on the gridiron, applications increase by 18.7%.

  b) To attain similar effects, a school has to either lower tuition by 3.8% or increase the quality of its education by recruiting higher-quality faculty who are paid 5% more than their average peers in the academic labor market.

c) Students with lower than average SAT scores tend to have a stronger preference for schools known for athletic success, while students with higher SAT scores prefer institutions with greater academic quality.

d) Students with lower academic prowess value the success of intercollegiate athletics for longer periods of time than the high SAT achievers. Even students with high SAT scores are significantly affected by athletic success—one of the biggest surprises from the research, Chung noted.

e) Schools become more academically selective with athletic success.

Each of these successes is directly attributable to the efforts of student-athletes who may not directly benefit from the net tuition revenue generated by the increased enrollment. Colleges and universities are like other businesses: they need to make a profit. Businesses compensate those who help them make a profit with a salary, commission, bonus, or other monetary incentive.

There are a few questions we must ask as we look at the issues we are discussing in this book. What purpose does athletics serve? Is its purpose to advance the mission of the institution? Is it to drive enrollment? Is it to supplement the student experience? Is it really about providing more participation opportunities or some combination of the above? In the case of many Power Five institutions, they are so large that the enrollment effect of a few intercollegiate athletics teams would be minimal at best.

- **Academic success and persistence**. Students who are underprepared academically for college are at a disadvantage when taking into consideration the hours they will practice and the rigors of college academics. This disadvantage may cause them to struggle academically and not graduate contributing to a loss of lifetime earnings potential.

- **Subsidizing non-revenue sports while receiving the same athletic aid packages.** Some student-athletes in revenue sports at Power Five institutions are subsidizing other sports programs that generate little or no income and may even operate at a loss. Many of these student-athletes in the non-revenue sports that students in football and basketball may be helping to subsidize are also receiving the same athletics aid package. Some are receiving a total cost of attendance package. Think about this for a moment in your workplace. We do not want to classify student-athletes as employees; however, can you think of a business model that pays employees who generate income for a business while also paying others who do not generate any revenue the same compensation?
- **Use of an agent.** Student-athletes cannot contract with an agent to help guide them on professional opportunities to maximize their earning potential until after they leave college. Other students have the ability to consult with or contract with a professional while enrolled in college regarding employment opportunities outside of a professional athletic career after college.
- **Uncompensated use of a student-athlete's photo or name**. According to the NCAA, NCAA Bylaw 12.5.2.1, after becoming a student-athlete, an individual shall not be eligible for participation in intercollegiate athletics if the individual:

    (a) Accepts any remuneration for or permits the use of his or her name or picture to advertise, recommend, or promote directly the sale or use of a commercial product or service of any kind; or
    (b) Receives remuneration for endorsing a commercial product or service through the individual's use of such product or service.

These are just a few of the many ways that some student-athletes are exploited, treated unfairly, or taken advantage in the present system of college sports.

CHAPTER 2

Life on the Plantation, Where the Exploited Generate and Support the Rest of the Plantation

S EVERAL BOOKS AND articles have been written about how the present structure of athletics at the Division I level closely resembles a plantation not only in structure, but also racially (Hawkins, 2010). I cringe at the comparison to slavery, but in some ways, it is similar.

Division I college athletics function as individual plantations with the organization functioning as the ultimate slave master. Within the plantation, you had a number of masters, overseers, and free labor. There are not many differences from what slavery used to be, except the races, genders, and titles of those controlling the plantation and laborers have changed. Today, the masters could be called university president, AD, head coach, assistant coach, offensive coordinator, academic advisor.

Today's exploited student-athletes are much more diverse than the slaves that once provided the free forced labor on plantations. They are Black and White, gay and straight, Christian, Catholic, Protestant, Muslim, Hindu, and Buddhist. The exploited come from rich families and poor families, from cities, suburbs, and rural areas. Some of the exploited have two parents; others are from single parent homes.

One thing that has not changed much is that the field labor still looks pretty much as it did in the early 1800s. Students of color are providing the labor that drives Division I athletics in revenue sports while subsidizing the operations of the rest of the plantation. The biggest difference today is that some of the exploited actually have more power and influence than they realize. In some cases, revenue sports equal power. Non-revenue sports equal no power.

To put part of this issue into perspective, let me share with you the story of Jayden.

Meet Jayden

I want to share my experience speaking with a former Division I African American student-athlete. I will not use his real name, but I will call him Jayden. Jayden was only a few years removed from his time on the plantation and agreed to let me share parts of his experience as a Division I basketball player at a Power Five institution as long as I did not use his name, mention his school, or his coach by name.

As part of my research for this book and a previous study, I had the opportunity to interview Jayden on several occasions. The more I spoke to Jayden, the more I began to understand how common his story was.

Let me give you a bit of background on Jayden. Jayden was an all-state player in Illinois and played for an extremely successful high school program in the Chicago area. He was a highly recruited prospect ranked in the top 100 nationally by many scouting services. Following his senior year, Jayden decided to attend a Power Five member institution in the east. Jayden mentioned that part of his decision to attend this institution was playing close to an NBA market and the members of the coaching staff talking about how they had helped previous student-athletes get drafted into the NBA and others that had obtained contracts overseas.

Jayden admitted that he was not sure what he wanted to study when he enrolled, but ended up majoring in communications, as many of his teammates and other student-athletes did. To me, this was a bit concerning and a clear case of clustering, which I will touch on a little later.

At 6'9," Jaden was a versatile college player who was confortable playing with his back to the basket at center or away from the basket at the power forward position. He mentioned that on numerous occasions his head coach and members of the coaching staff suggested that if he were going to play at the "next level" evolving to a true "Stretch-4" would be key for Jayden.

After 4 years and four NCAA tournament appearances, Jayden had exhausted his eligibility and returned home to the Chicago area many credit hours short of his degree. He was not drafted and had bounced around the world in many professional basketball leagues in Europe and South America. I asked Jayden why he did not return to the Power Five institution and finish his degree. In his words, "It was almost like when I was done playing for them and had no more eligibility, they didn't have much use for me. They were concerned more about getting returning players ready for next season and recruiting new players."

I was heartbroken listening to what Jayden told me about his treatment from the coaching staff and the institution. Nobody at the institution ever followed up with him about completing his degree. This institution even offered an online degree completion program!

When I asked how he felt about his time and experiences at the Power Five institution, Jayden stated that he enjoyed his time playing ball, liked his coaches, enjoyed the tournament appearances, and his teammates. He shared that he hated not having much money and missed some of the things "normal" students did because he was either practicing, traveling, or some other activity related to playing basketball. Jayden did say that he was on a "full ride" and left the Power Five institution with no debt, but it was little consolation for not having a degree. Keep in mind that Jayden was more than academically prepared for the rigors of college and being a Division I athlete based on his preparation at a good high school; more than meeting NCAA qualifier standards, and high-standardized test scores.

As Jayden and I left what was our third meeting, I asked him how he and his girlfriend Sheila were doing. At this point, Jayden told me that Sheila is pregnant. They are having a little girl, and he may not try to play ball anywhere next season so he can be close to family and find work to support them. While Jayden had made some money playing professional basketball overseas after college, he admitted that he had not been as smart as he should have been with his money. Without a degree, his options are limited, but Jayden and Sheila are hopeful that he might find a job to support them.

Jayden's story is a perfect example of what is wrong with Division I athletics, and he is certainly not alone, as his story continues to play out each season, year after year, not only for football and basketball players, but also for student-athletes in many other Division I sports.

Jayden's Power Five institution is one of 50 or so plantations that have basketball revenues that exceed expenses each year. When you take into account football, his former institution is one of about 25 that are self-sufficient because of the combined success of their football and men's basketball programs. His former institution also subsidizes the operations of all of the non-revenue sports that lose money each year and whose rosters are comprised primarily of White student-athletes. Jayden even mentioned that he and his teammates would occasionally talk about how some of the "minor sports" would not even exist if it were not for football and basketball.

Ironically, none of the head coaches of any of the athletic teams at Jayden's institution are African American. African American student-athletes lead the men's basketball team. The longer Jayden was at a Power Five institution, the more he began to understand the system and how he was being used. "Everyone thinks the scholarship makes things even," he said.

Jayden shared with me the feelings that he and some of his teammates had about being taken advantage of and not being valued as anything more than basketball players in the system. Without Jayden and his African American teammates, chances were that his team would not have made the NCAA tournament and have "any shot" at winning a national championship. His words, not mine. Even more interesting was Jayden's comments on how the roster was comprised and the roles of each player on the team.

By our third conversation, Jayden seemed to be more comfortable with the topic and really opened up about things behind the scenes and what he called the "real deal." He said, "Without us, we don't sell out all of our home games in our 17,000-seat arena generating millions for the athletics department." Jayden continued, "Without us and the football team, a lot of White kids don't have an opportunity to participate in lacrosse, soccer, gymnastics, volleyball, softball, golf, tennis, or swimming and diving here."

Each student participating in the previously mentioned sports has at least some of their athletic aid provided by the efforts of Jayden and his teammates. These African American student-athletes generate revenue that pays a portion of the salaries for the coaching staffs and operational budgets for a dozen or more sports that will lose money every year they exist. My point here is that Jayden's example is typical at Power Five institutions for many African Americans who play football or basketball.

The quickest way to enact change with the NCAA Power Five institutions, conference commissioners, AD's, coaches, is to hit them where it hurts—their wallets. Without the African American student-athlete, there just is no "big time" NCAA Division I football or basketball as we know it today. It would be hard to justify highly compensated coaches and administrators based on what the potential product on the field and court might look like.

I am in no way saying that White student-athletes that compete in football and basketball are not highly skilled, talented, dedicated, and committed. I mention these only because the majority of student-athletes competing in football and basketball at the top Division I level are African American (Lapchick, 2017). This is where the majority of the revenue is generated, where the bulk of the power and influence lies. Imagine what these sports would look like if many the most talented African American students took their skills and talents elsewhere?

CHAPTER 3

Why African American Students Should Care

EACH PROSPECTIVE AND current Division I African American student-athlete bears some responsibility in pushing for change and reform. These students are responsible for helping to make things better for those who will compete in intercollegiate athletics at the Division I level after them. To whom much is given, much is required and much is expected! The right thing to do is to make things better for those who will come later.

African American student-athletes must leave their house in better order than they found it, and those who follow must do the same. Part of making things better is using collective numbers to influence change and reform. The reform and changes that are needed go beyond just whether student-athletes who help generate revenue should receive a portion of it.

For the African American student-athlete competing in a revenue sport, he or she must leverage their talents to help make needed changes to NCAA Division I athletics. These changes not only promote fair revenue distribution, but they will also indirectly improve graduation rates and the overall student-athlete experience.

African American student-athletes must ask themselves many questions during the recruiting process and look at the decision they are going to make about what college or university they will attend to continue their education and compete at athletically as part of the bigger picture in terms of reforming the exploitative system.

African American student-athletes are good enough to be recruited in disproportionate numbers in the revenue sports, but African

Americans are under represented in coaching and administrative roles at all levels of intercollegiate athletics. The biggest underrepresentation of African American head coaches and administrators is at the Division I level (Lapchick, 2017). African American students have an obligation to do their part in making the needed changes in governance, revenue distribution, and hiring practices.

As I've mentioned and will continue to mention, I'm all for hiring the best person for the job as well as institutions and head coaches hiring who they want as administrators and members of their coaching staffs. African American head football and basketball coaches are under represented in all NCAA divisions. They have had a harder time securing head coaching positions in Division I football and basketball and are more likely to be fired than their White counterparts (Kopkin, 2014). African Americans are equally as underrepresented in administration across all NCAA divisions (Lapchick, 2017), "but it stands out much more in Division I" (p. 4).

I'm not asking for something similar to the NFL's Rooney rule, because I don't think it will be necessary once African American prospective student-athletes start wielding their collective power and influence. But just imagine the affect these students could have if they began taking their talent and skill to non-Power Five institutions, Historically Black Colleges and Universities (HBCUs), the NAIA, NCAA Division II, and NCAA Division III.

The effect on a shift away from "big-time" Division I Power Five programs would be felt within just a few years. Some of the top programs in Division I football, and men and women's basketball would look vastly different. I am not saying it would cripple them, but the difference on the field and court would be very noticeable.

What if football powers like Alabama, Clemson, Notre Dame, and Ohio State could not attract and sign the highly rated recruiting classes they traditionally have. What would UConn, Kentucky, Duke, or Villanova look like without the many highly rated African American recruits that have attended these blueblood institutions over the years? In as little as 2-3 years, the effect of just a few hundred of the top rated recruits in football, men's basketball, and women's basketball making a radical decision to take their talents elsewhere would change the college football playoff and both NCAA Division I basketball tournaments.

Can you picture a college football playoff expanded to eight teams hypothetically with UCF, Houston, Boise State, Western Michigan, South Florida, Memphis, Georgia Southern, Navy and Temple? What about a men's basketball final four with North Carolina Central, Tennessee State, Belmont, and IUPUI? A women's final four with no UConn, Notre Dame, Baylor, or South Carolina would be unthinkable, but a very real possibility. The affect could be more significant in women's basketball because of the differences in talent and resources that the top programs have compared to mid- and low-major programs. You could realistically have a women's Division I final four with teams such as UW Green Bay, South Dakota St., Mercer, and Florida Gulf Coast.

Now, this concept will be hard to grasp by many African American prospective student-athletes, and some will not consider any other institution outside of a Power Five institution to continue their education and display their talents. However, there will be others that believe that the only way to the NFL, NBA, or WNBA is to attend an institution under the present system of governance where they are exploited, revenue is not distributed fairly, and graduation rates for African American student-athletes are lower than those of their White student-athlete peers (Bauer-Wolf, 2018).

A recent article that appeared in *Inside Higher Ed* reported the narrative that the NCAA assertions regarding African American males graduating at higher rates isn't true according to Executive Director Shaun R. Harper of the University of Southern California's Center on Race and Equity. Harper's study shows that there is still much work to do despite what the NCAA wants to report and say in its commercials (Harper, 2018).

According to the article, Harper's report found, at worse, the truth is being stretched. While across the board in Division I, African-American male athletes do graduate in higher percentages than African-American men who don't play sports, that's not the case with the 65 institutions that comprise the Power Five conferences, the NCAA's wealthiest leagues: the Atlantic Coast, Big Ten, Big 12, Pac-12, and Southeastern Conferences. These are the colleges most in the sports spotlight that for decades have dominated football and men's basketball championships" (Harper, 2018).

A little more than 55% of African American male athletes at the Power Five institutions graduate within six years versus 60% of African American males overall in the undergraduate population and about 76% of all undergraduates. Only three institutions in the Power Five, The University of Louisville, Mississippi State University, and the University of Utah have graduated African American male student-athletes at rates higher than or equal to their undergraduate populations" (Harper, 2018).

The amount of influence that just a few hundred African American student-athletes could have on changing the landscape of intercollegiate athletics across all divisions and associations goes far beyond the football playoff and the basketball final fours. If institutions want to treat student-athletes like employees but do not want to pay them, African American student-athletes should consider organizing like other student groups and organizations.

Following the model and mission of the Student-Athlete Advisory Council (SAAC), African American student-athletes could use a similarly structured organization as a platform to give a voice to issues and create a direct line to institutions and the NCAA. No longer would empty talk about reform, improving graduation rates, fair distribution of revenue, and other issues central to African American student-athletes be discussed without a group at the table representing those who are supplying the labor that drives the NCAA and its member institutions. Like any credible and respected organization, this group would elect leadership, hold regular meetings, and vote on membership issues separate from the NCAA or any institution.

The membership of this organization would not be limited to African American student-athletes. Membership could include any student-athlete from all NCAA divisions, the NAIA, NJCAA, USCAA, and any other intercollegiate governing associations. There really is no limit to the causes that this group could use their power to implement change. Forcing a new distribution of revenue model could be one of the first challenges for this group.

As I mentioned before I will share one model I think could be the foundation for these talks. This group could be the catalyst for some significant changes outside of revenue generation. The majority of the affect this group could have would influence more than just African American student-athletes.

One idea this group could consider is for all students in revenue sports being permitted to reduce the course load student-athletes are required to take during their season and fund a 5th or even a 6th year of eligibility. The additional funding could be provided in lieu of any stipend that the students may be receiving in their first four years of attendance.

One way to provide the additional funding for students needing a 5th or 6th year of attendance to graduate could be to use a portion of the funds that are accumulated using the model I propose later in the book.

CHAPTER 4

Ways African American Student-Athletes Can Empower Themselves in the Present Structure

THE CURRENT STRUCTURE of intercollegiate athletics in NCAA Division I—more specifically the revenue sports of football, men's basketball and women's basketball—is designed to benefit institutions and not the students who comprise the majority of the rosters in these sports. Any African American student-athlete competing at the Division I level in these sports should be concerned about the potential revenue they are generating for their institution above the value of their athletic aid. Here are 11 things I believe an African American prospective student-athlete considering competing at the Division I level should consider in order to empower themselves.

1. Refuse to be field labor for the plantation. Student-athletes at the University of Missouri in 2015 proved that just the threat of a boycott at the institutional level could have an enormous affect. This threatened boycott showed us several things. Changes do not have to occur slowly and that collectively the student-athletes truly have the power to enact change. By merely threatening to boycott a single game in 2015, the students from the University of Missouri football team stood with other non-student-athletes, faculty, and staff over the climate on campus and other issues. In less than two days, University of Missouri President Tim

Wolfe resigned and the upcoming game versus BYU was no longer in jeopardy of not being played (Silverman, 2015).

Imagine the power of African American student-athletes boycotting a home football conference opener at a Power Five institution? What if these students stood shoulder to should with their non-African American student-athlete teammates to boycott just a single game such as a conference championship, bowl game, NCAA basketball tournament game or a game in the final four? I really don't think that I'd need to continue writing here about the other 14 suggestions I have if African American student-athletes conducted or threatened to conduct a strategic boycott where it would hurt the NCAA and Power Five institutions the most.

The two places these students could potentially inflict the most damage and have the largest platform would be during the four-team bowl subdivision playoff or the opening round of the men's division I basketball tournament, March madness. I know that there are many students (including African American) who would not participate in such a boycott and I completely get it as a former student-athlete, college coach, and AD. However, what happened at the University of Missouri gives us just a glimpse of what is possible.

My advice to student-athletes is do not accept conditional academic acceptance to an institution. I mention this as being high on my list for a couple of reasons. Playing a sport at the Division I level is already hard enough. College academics are also difficult and take significant preparation and commitment. Accepting anything other than unconditional admission could be setting any student-athlete up for failure. Unfortunately, this is commonplace at the Division I level in football and basketball and is disproportionately applied to African American student-athletes in revenue sports (Mitchell, 2017).

One of the areas that non-student-athletes complain about when talking about the athletics aid and other so called perks that student-athletes receive is preferential treatment when it comes to admissions. If we look at admitting student-athletes at Power Five institutions with more weight being placed on academic merit first, what would football and basketball rosters look like?

Frequently, student-athletes who are underprepared academically to play a sport at the Division I level and handle the academic rigor of college are admitted conditionally. This not only sets students-athletes up for failure, but it also fuels animosity towards student-athletes in general from non-student-athletes (sometimes other student-athletes not receiving full aid), and faculty. It also affects African American student-athletes more frequently because these student-athletes are more likely to be recruited and admitted to an institution underprepared to succeed in college.

Admitting many student-athletes who are underprepared for the academics in college, along with participating in a Division I sport, has often been done with the assumption that resources are in place to help these students succeed academically, remain eligible, and graduate. Is it fair to be recruited to a Power Five or Division I institution in a revenue sport strung along about the possibility of making it to the NFL, NBA, or WNBA? This is a common scenario for those who are not among the 2% or fewer who may get a shot at the pros. Alumni, ADs, coaches, and their peers are telling these student-athletes that the athletic aid they receive should be compensation enough while the institution, the NCAA, and the Power Five member institutions continue to make billions of dollars (Joiner, 2016).

2. Prospective African American student-athletes should do their homework regarding graduation rates before verbally committing to an institution or signing a letter of intent. The prospective student-athlete and their family should research the graduation rates for African American student-athletes in their sport and for those in all sports at any institution they are considering attending. Research the graduation rates for all African American students compared to all White students as well as African American student-athletes compared to White student-athletes. If the graduation rate at an institution where an African American student is considering enrolling is more than 10% lower than that of White students, this should be seen as a red flag. This institution should be avoided at all cost no matter how slick the sales pitch is by the head coach and his or her staff. This is a clear and blatant sign of exploitation. This scenario, despite reforms already put in place, is more common that you think, but this information will never be disclosed during the recruiting process.

The questions that prospective African American student-athletes and their family should ask before making any commitment are, "What is the graduation rate for African American student-athletes?" What is the graduation rate for African American student-athletes in football, men's basketball, etc." In a 2017 documentary on *The Undefeated*, by Derrick Jackson, it was reported that 24 Power Five conference member institutions graduated less than 50% of their African American student-athletes in football and men's basketball. Jackson (2017) said, "If you include not-so-big-time Division I programs, the landscape is littered with many more schools from California to Florida that are below 50% for African-American athletes in either men's basketball or football or women's track" (Jackson, 2017, para.6.)

Keep in mind that the Power Five conferences are comprised of 65 teams. So just taking into account men's revenue sports, 36.9% of these institutions continue to earn significant revenue based on the sacrifices, blood, and sweat of African American student-athletes while less than 50% of them graduate. Let us look for a moment at how this potentially affects each of the men's revenue sports.

If you consider that the maximum number of athletics scholarships that can be awarded for football in Division I are 85 and African Americans account for 55.9% of students on Division I football rosters, each team could have approximately 47 African American players (Lapchick, 2017). Approximately 23 of these students will not graduate for each Power Five member institution.

Looking at men's basketball, there are 13 athletics scholarships that can be awarded. If African American student-athletes account for 53% of students on Division I men's basketball rosters, each team could have six or seven African American players. Approximately three or four of these students will not graduate for each Power Five member institution.

3. Consider attending HBCUs. While I'm certainly not going to try to promote HBUCs and predominantly White institution (PWIs) over one another, I do believe both types of institutions are important, and each has a different value depending on what any one student is seeking in their academic and athletics experience. I personally do not believe you can compare HBCUs, Hispanic Serving Institutions (HSIs), and PWIs. Each has a different mission as well as unique differences, advantages, and disadvantages depending on the student.

The feeling of cultural and social isolation that some African American students can feel on campuses of large PWIs is something they will not experience at an HBCU. This can be common among some African American student-athletes at PWIs because of the amount of time they spend on their sport and with their teammates. My goal is to help empower the African American student-athletes. That means helping them find a way to earn a degree in an area of their choosing that supports their career goals and allows them to compete in the sport of their choice without being exploited. Until reforms are made at the Division I level in the revenue sports, all options should be on the table.

For the sake of this book, again, my focus is just on the elite (those who have the potential to make money in their sport as a professional, NFL, NBA, etc.) African American student-athlete. Historically, Black colleges and universities or HBCUs in today's political, social, and exploitive climate in intercollegiate athletics are an option that prospective African American student-athletes must seriously consider. Most HBCU's are mission-based institutions offering a high quality education welcoming to all students regardless of race. All races and ethnicities are represented on HBCU campuses, and many provide an outstanding educational experience.

Students attending HBCUs have the benefit of supportive and caring faculty and staff (not to say they don't at PWIs) that are creating a specialized educational experience just for African Americans. This not only builds in a support system, but it also does just what the purpose of this book is about: Empowering African American students not only athletically, but also in a way that creates a graduate who is ready to be a leader and tackle today's real world challenges.

In addition to the educational experience that HBCUs can provide are the opportunities in intercollegiate athletics. At the time of publication of this book, there were 23 HBCUs that competed at the Division I level. Note all Division I HBCUs offering football compete in the FCS (Football Championship Subdivision), formerly known as I-AA. The FCS has produced notable NFL stars such as Carson Wentz who was the second overall NFL draft pick by the Philadelphia Eagles in 2016, Joe Flacco, Antoine Bethea, and Dominique Rodgers-Cromartie. The institutions and their conference affiliation are listed below.

Southwestern Athletics Conference (SWAC)
Alabama A&M University
Alabama State University
Alcorn State University
University of Arkansas-Pine Bluff
Grambling State University
Jackson State University
Mississippi Valley State University
Prairie View A&M University
Southern University
Texas Southern University

Mid Atlantic Athletic Conference (MEAC)
Bethune-Cookman University
Coppin State University
Delaware State University
Florida A&M University
Howard University
University of Maryland Eastern Shore
Morgan State University
Norfolk State University
North Carolina A&T State University
North Carolina Central University
South Carolina State University

Big South Conference
Hampton University

Ohio Valley Conference
Tennessee State University

4. Consider other alternatives outside of the Power Five and NCAA Division I. There are even more intercollegiate participation opportunities not just for elite African American student-athletes, but also for all student-athletes in Division II, Division III, the NAIA, and USCAA institutions, which I will discuss shortly. African American student-athletes may find learning and competing with large numbers of students that look like them as well as faculty and athletics coaches and administrators as a factor in their college choice. Some students may find this comforting and a contributor to their academic success. Later in the book, I will give some examples of those who have attended HBCUs and gone on to professional careers in the NFL and NBA.

I'll finish my thoughts on HBCUs with this: One of the selling points that some coaches will use in their recruiting pitch to African American PSAs is that their institution has and will continue to provide poor African American students with an opportunity to get out of their "hood," earn an education they may not have had an opportunity to get, and provide exposure for the pros. I will not dispute most of these pitches, as I'm all for providing opportunity to those who may not have had it otherwise; however, HBCUs graduate more poorer African American students than PWIs (Nichols & Evans-Bell, 2017).

5. Consider an Empower University. If an African American student-athlete is truly elite and has a future in continuing their sport professionally, I believe his or her talent is going to give him or her an opportunity to realize their dream no matter at what level they compete. I urge these students and their families to weigh carefully how big of an influence the level of competition they will be facing each week truly influences their development and exposure, and ultimately their ability to be drafted or make money as a professional.

As I mentioned previously, if a student-athlete has the ability to compete professionally, it will not matter at which level or at what type of institution that student-athlete competed. Their skills and talents will continue to be developed at the professional level.

Now, back to Empower universities. So maybe an HBCU or HSI is not for a particular African American student-athlete. No problem. I have another suggestion on how African American student-athletes can put more power in their hands and remove the issue of exploitation almost entirely while achieving the truest most organic sense of being a student-athlete. So, you are probably saying to yourself, "What does he mean by an Empower university, I've never heard of one of these?" Yes you have! In my eyes, an Empower university is any non-Division I institution including members of the NAIA (National Association of Intercollegiate Athletics), NCAA, Division II, and NCAA Division III.

Again, I am limiting the discussion to those elite African American student-athletes in the revenue sports of football, men's basketball, and women's basketball. Stay with me here. If an African American student-athlete has the potential to get drafted or have a professional career, let's agree on one thing for the suggestion I'm making: we can assume these students are going to get their opportunity in the NFL, NBA, WNBA, etc., regardless of where they get their college education. If the talent and ability is there, these students will be on someone's radar with how scouting and prospect identification has evolved today.

That being said, does it really matter where these student-athletes get their education? Does it really matter that they may not be competing against the best competition week in and week out? Now I know what some will say about the benefits of competing at the highest level against the best competition in the "big time" world of Division I intercollegiate athletics. I get it, and I truly understand as a former college basketball coach and someone who was paid to play basketball after college, that the best preparation, the best resources, and competing against the best competition makes a student-athlete better. I cannot argue this, but this book is not intended to argue where the best competition is.

My objective is to help as many African American student-athletes graduate from college, minimize or eliminate their exploitation, begin the career of their choice, and help position them for becoming a professional athlete if that is where opportunity, talent, and ability should take them.

Let me give a brief overview on the missions and philosophies of the other associations and divisions I have mentioned as alternatives to NCAA Division I for African American student-athletes.

The NAIA was founded in 1937, and according to their website, they provide 65,000 student-athletes the opportunity to play college sports at over 250-member institutions. The NAIA seeks to enhance the character building aspects of sports and is committed to promoting this mission through the core values of integrity, respect, responsibility, sportsmanship, and servant leadership. The NAIA has a history of being a trailblazing association by being the first collegiate athletics association to invite HBCUs into membership and the first collegiate association to sponsor both men's and women's national championships (NAIA, n.d.).

NAIA member institutions have enrollments as small as 500 students at some faith-based members and up to several thousand students at many of the public institutions. While few NAIA member institutions offer "full rides," a partial athletics aid model is common where a student would typically receive a combination of athletics, merit, and need-based aid in their financial package. As with all associations and divisions, an NAIA member institutions has scholarship/athletics aid limits per sport set by the association.

At one time, the NCAA's own website said, "The NCAA was formed in 1906 as an association to protect young people from the dangerous and exploitive athletics practices of the time" (NCAA, n.d.). The link to this information was www.wps/wcm/connect/public/NCAA/About the NCAA/History. Now (as of 2018) the website shows "page not found" when you try to retrieve it. I mention this because I found the link was working when I was conducting research for my dissertation years ago.

There are now three distinct divisions that make up the NCAA. Division II was formed in 1973. According to NCAA, Division II membership is comprised of over 300 colleges and universities with academic/athletics balance, and campus and community involvement as pillars of their philosophy. Although Division II doesn't have the financial resources that Division I member institutions do, the NCAA website says Division II student-athletes are just as competitive and in many cases just as skilled as their Division I counterparts, but institutions in Division II generally don't have the financial resources to devote to their athletics programs or choose not to place such a heavy financial emphasis on them. Enrollments at Division II schools range from fewer than 2,500 students to more than 25,000. According to the NCAA, about 87% of its member schools have fewer than 8,000 students.

NCAA Division III is the largest division of the NCAA and may be best known for offering no athletics aid/scholarships. Over 180,000 student-athletes at 450 institutions participate in intercollegiate athletics in the division. According to NCAA "Academics are the primary focus for Division III student-athletes. The division minimizes the conflicts between athletics and academics and helps student-athletes progress toward graduation through shorter practice and playing seasons and regional competition that reduces time away from academic studies. Participants are integrated on campus and treated like all other members of the student body, keeping them focused on being a student first" (NCAA, n.d., para. 2).

Item number three of the NCAA Division III philosophy statement says, "Shall not award financial aid to any student on the basis of athletics leadership, ability, participation or performance." While I'm only pointing out item number three, the Division III philosophy has many components related to competition, equity, diversity, academics, finance, budgets, admissions, and other areas that really could and should apply to all divisions and associations. The Division III philosophy statement is certainly an interesting read considering the state of intercollegiate athletics in general and what Division I has become. As of the publication of this book the statement can be found at http://www.ncaa.org/governance/division-iii-philosophy-statement

6. Request a 4-year financial aid agreement issued by the institution from the financial aid department and not the athletics

department. This agreement would be more beneficial to a student-athlete than a restrictive and binding Letter of Intent. The concept of financial aid agreements is new but gaining popularity because they do not tie a student-athlete to one particular institution. The financial aid agreement moves the power to the student-athlete so they are not tied to an institution should it not work out for them for numerous reasons.

The financial aid agreement can be signed at anytime, and the institution is obligated to the terms of the agreement whether the student competes as an athlete or not. That is the key for the prospective student-athlete and their family. Essentially the student could sign as many financial aid agreements as he or she wanted so that they make the absolute best choice for them with no pressure. The prospective student-athlete can take his or her time to make a decision on where he or she wants to attend without worrying about signing periods and their associated deadlines. The financial aid agreement really gives the student time to thoroughly weigh all options.

Signing a Letter of Intent stops the recruiting process and does not allow a student to keep exploring other institutions that may be better for them. Signing a financial aid agreement with multiple institutions also can allow a prospective student-athlete to wait on an institution that may not have offered them an athletics aid package. For example, if Billy wants to attend Institution A but they have not made him an offer, he could sign financial aid agreements with Institutions B, C, D, and E, and wait for his first choice. If he never gets an offer from Institution A, he may be able to go to one of his other choices.

Signing a financial aid agreement almost assures the student-athlete that he or she will continue to be recruited by schools on their list and others because the agreement allows recruitment to continue. Signing a Letter of Intent ends the recruiting process. The best part is that the potential student-athlete has maintained control of the process and made the best decision without rushing, and being committed by signing a Letter of Intent.

In full disclosure, there is the possibility that none of a student-athlete's options will be available if they wait too long, so there can be a risk that is not present with a Letter of Intent. A Letter of Intent can be nearly impossible to get out of should the potential student-athlete change his or her mind, the head coach that recruited them leaves, or other reasons.

In some instances where a student may be released from their Letter of Intent, it often comes at a high price with restrictions on where a student can or cannot transfer. Additionally, if the student-athlete is at the Division I level, they will most likely under current rules have to sit out a year if transferring to another Division I institution. There have been some ugly cases in the last few years where African American student-athletes have asked for a release from their Letter of Intent. Keep in mind that coaches and administrators can freely quit at one institution and take a position at another whenever they choose with no restrictions.

At the Division I level, student-athletes are not afforded this luxury and in fact, they are penalized twice for asking for a release. They are often penalized by their current institution with transfer restrictions and then by the NCAA, which will typically require the student-athlete to sit out a year if transferring to another Division I institution.

For example, according to a 2017 *USA Today* article in one recent high profile case, "Kansas State football player Corey Sutton initially was denied permission to contact any of the 35 schools he said he had requested, and called Wildcats' coach Bill Snyder a 'slave master' in a tweet. Snyder publicly defended his decision not to grant Sutton's request, but Kansas State relented shortly afterward, freeing up Sutton to transfer to Appalachian State"(Schroder, 2017, para. 3). The author also noted that the NCAA even has a group exploring the possibility of creating a rule that would control where a student-athlete could transfer to if they wanted a release from their LOI.

The aforementioned example and others like it only confirm why African American student-athletes in revenue sports must seize each and every opportunity to empower themselves in everything related to their intercollegiate athletics experience. The institutions and the NCAA certainly are not looking out for their best interests as evidenced by the example above and the whole concept of the Letter of Intent.

One final thought here is that student-athletes must be aware of the terms of their financial aid agreement or athletics aid package. Ideally, the student-athlete is looking for a 4-year or longer commitment in writing. Typically, athletics aid packages are for 1-year terms and annually renewable at the discretion of the head coach. This means that in the case of a change of heart by the coach, injury, or other reasons, a student-athlete's aid package may not be renewed after the initial award. Some Division I institutions have gone away from this practice by offering student-athletes a 4-year athletics aid package.

7. Don't be afraid to say no to an institution where there are few students, faculty, staff, coaches and athletics department leaders that look like you. African American student-athletes who compete in revenue sports at PWIs should not feel as if they need to try to be anything but themselves and that is a proud African American student. African American student-athletes who are not student-athletes have expressed frustration about attending PWIs and feeling that the color of their skin was a problem for many of their fellow students and even some faculty and staff (Whaley, 2013).

Being an African American student should not be a problem for anyone, but the fact is that it is a problem for some on many college campuses. What I'm asking is that African American students and their families empower themselves and not even consider attending and participating in a sport at an institution that has had a history of racial incidents and lacks diversity. There are too many other places that a prospective African American student-athlete can choose from that are truly inclusive, welcoming, and reflective of the diversity of our society today. These institutions also represent diversity in their athletic departments with women and people of color in leadership positions and not just football or basketball coaches. More on this in a bit.

Today's political climate has created a volatile environment on college campuses where people feel like they can say whatever they want and in many cases do what they want. Also in this climate, comments and actions that not long ago were clearly deemed as racist, morally, culturally, and politically unacceptable are now the norm. I mention this to say that the reality is that at many Power Five institutions there are a significant number of students, student-athletes, coaches, athletics administrators, faculty, and even institutional leadership that only value "the African American student" for their athletic ability if they value them at all. At the same time, many of these same people simply don't want African American or any students of color there and assume many of these students wouldn't be there if they were not a student-athlete. Let us call it what it is. And that is that the climate on the campuses at many PWI's is just plain toxic.

In just the first five months of 2018, the "Journal of Blacks in Higher Education" (2018) reported on nearly a dozen campus racial incidents. Three of these incidents reported were from Power Five member institutions. At the University of Oregon, racist graffiti was found written on sidewalks, racist flyers and signs were posted on the campus of the University of South Carolina, and a White student at the University of Alabama was expelled for posting racist videos. These are just a very very small sample of the type of hate that not only African American students are facing, but all students of color. These incidents are examples of why African American student-athletes must do their homework during the recruiting process and get a feel for the climate they may be walking into. They have an obligation to themselves and to all future African American students, not just student-athletes who will follow after them.

This type of due diligence is essential for any African American student-athlete considering attending a Power Five institution. No longer can these students fall for slick recruiting pitches from coaches representing institutions that may not value the African American student as a person, student, and the cultural diversity they bring. There are simply too many alternatives for the elite African American student-athlete to earn their degree and be in a position to make money in their sport.

While the world of intercollegiate athletics at any level is at times a bubble, this bubble is much larger and more pronounced on Division I campuses. To an extent, many African American student-athletes at Power Five institutions are insulated from some of the mess but not immune from it nor naïve to it (i.e., University of Missouri football player boycott). Keep in mind the incidents we hear about are only those that are reported and available as part of public information requests or those that make the national news. Far more incidents like those I cite occur on campuses all over the country that the general public never hears about.

As someone who has worked on college campuses of all sizes, including PWIs and HBCUs for nearly 20 years, I can say first hand there is so much that goes on that is kept quiet and hidden from the public to protect the institution from scrutiny and judgment. Racial incidents, sexual assaults, discrimination, and crimes too numerous to mention.

8. Prospective African American student-athletes must pay close attention to the make up of head coach, leadership, and decision-making positions at any institution they are considering during the recruiting process. I am going to throw a significant amount of data at you here, but I think the numbers will reinforce my point. According to the "2017 College Sport Racial & Gender Report Card," African Americans, people of color, and women are extremely underrepresented in leadership and head coaching positions at the Division I level with little or no progress being made to improve (Lapchick, 2017).

By continuing to attend these institutions as an African American student-athlete, they are indirectly allowing many of the Power Five institutions as well as institutions in Division II and Division III to continue hiring practices that keep African Americans, people of color, and women underrepresented in intercollegiate leadership and coaching positions. Speaking for a moment about revenue sports at Power Five institutions, we must ask ourselves why are African American students good enough to be recruited and comprise the majority of Division I football, men's basketball, and women's basketball rosters, but aren't good enough to hold leadership roles and head coaching roles at the same rates?

Lets look at the raw data on this and you can come to your own conclusion. Dr. Richard Lapchick is the director of The Institute for

Diversity & Ethics in Sports (TIDES) at the University of Central Florida. In February of 2018, TIDES released their 2017 report card and college sports received a C+ for its racial hiring practices. If you consider both college sports and professional sports, college sports has the lowest grade for racial and gender hiring practices despite having significantly more opportunities at the college level. Lapchick says in his report that, "Opportunities for coaches of color continued to be an area of significant concern in all divisions" (p. 3). Does anyone else have an issue here with underrepresentation in leadership and coaching positions and what could be seen as overrepresentation of African American student-athletes on Division I football, men's basketball and Women's basketball rosters? It just does not make sense that we are going to recruit the best for a roster, but college sport hiring practices are not always designed to identify and hire the best coaches. Simply hiring coaches that "look" like those who have maintained power and influence does not mean the best are being hired.

Again, according to the 2017 TIDES report, "86.5 % of Division I, 87.8% of Division II, and 91.6% of Division III men's coaches are White. On the women's side, Whites hold 84.5%, 86.8%, and 91% percent of coaching positions in Divisions I, II, and III, respectively"(p. 4). The report confirms what all prospective African American student-athletes should be concerned about and that is large numbers of African American students in Division I football, men's basketball, and women's basketball are coached by decreasing numbers of African American coaches, which is a problem.

As I mentioned earlier, African American students continuing to attend these Power Five institutions in such large numbers in revenue sports only makes some African American students indirectly complicit in their own exploitation as student-athletes and the poor hiring practices for College athletics leaders and coaches. The TIDES report also stated, "In men's Division I basketball, 22.3 % of all head coaches are African American, which is up 1.5 percentage points from the 20.8 % reported in the 2015-2016 season. That is down 2.9 percentage points from the all-time high of 25.2% reported in the 2005-2006 season. In all, 25%

percent of the Division I men's basketball coaches were coaches of color which is 1.8% percent more than in 2016" (p. 2).

The numbers were even worse for Division I women's basketball, where "African-American women head coaches held 11.4% of the positions in 2016-2017 and African-American men held 4.6% of the positions in 2016-2017 for a combined percentage of 16%. This was a decrease from the 16.8% reported in 2015-2016. As in other sports, the 11.4% African-American women head coaches stood in stark contrast to the 43.4% of the African-American women student-athletes who play basketball" (TIDES, 2017, p. 2).

TIDES data confirmed abysmal numbers for Division I football related to African American head coaches. "As of October, 2017, there were 130 head football coaches at FBS schools and of those, 113 (86.9%) were White males. There were 17 (13.1%) FBS head football coaches that were people of color, which increased by 0.6% from the 2016-2017 year: 10.8% of these coaches were African American" (p. 18).

In this same discussion, I think it is important to note as of the 2016-2017 academic year, Whites comprised the majority of AD positions at 86.1%, 87.4%, and 93.4% in Division I, Division II, and Division III respectively" (p. 5). The report provided some data that should not come as a surprise to anyone who has watched even a little Division I football or men's basketball.

According to TIDES, "of all student-athletes in Division I football at the FBS level during the 2017 year, 55.9% were African Americans, 39% were White, 2.2% were Latinos, Asian/Pacific Islanders, which represented 2.5%, and 0.4 % of male Division I football student-athletes were classified as 'other'" (p. 7). The numbers for Division I men and women's basketball was similar. "Of the total student-athletes in Division I men's basketball, African Americans accounted for 53% while White athletes accounted for 26.9%. "Of the total student-athletes in Division I women's basketball, African American athletes decreased from 45.4% in 2015- 2016 to 43.4% in 2016-2017. White athletes increased from 34.8% in 2015-2016 to 35.3% in 2016-2017" (p. 7).

The percentages of African Americans represented in other leadership positions such as associate AD, assistant AD, senior women's administrator, faculty athletics representative, and sports information director, shows the same underrepresentation as AD positions at the Division I level (TIDES, 2017).

I know I've included a lot of numbers here, but I want to show another perspective on why prospective African American student-athletes who may play a revenue sport at the Division I level need to think carefully about their choices and the effect of their decision to attend a Power Five or Division I institution. The decision goes farther than just where a student will potentially earn a degree from and where they will play a sport. The data shows one way in which the exploitation manifests itself beyond the field of competition and long after any one African American student-athlete has competed in their sport.

9. Choose a major based on your career objectives. Do not be pressured into a perceived easy major or a major you are not interested in that has a disproportionate number of student-athletes represented. Avoid being a victim of *clustering* at all costs. Clustering is defined as having a large percentage of student-athletes from one sports team that have selected a particular major (Mitchell, 2017). Many institutions, not just Power Five members, engage in steering some student-athletes (not just African Americans) to certain majors. This may happen for several reasons. It could be to help certain students maintain eligibility or to manipulate graduation rates.

In a 2012 article in the "Lawrence Journal World," Shaun Hittle explored clustering in the Big 12. Citing an in depth Journal World study on Big 12 athletics, significant cases of clustering were identified. These included the Baylor football team. Fifty-one percent of players major in general studies compared with just 1% of all other undergraduates. According to Baylor's website, the program is designed for the general career areas of health, fitness, recreation, and sports. For Texas A & M, 37% of the men's basketball players and football players major in agricultural leadership and development, compared with less than 1%

of non-athletes. For Iowa State, seven of eleven men's basketball players majored in liberal studies (Hittle, 2012).

When you examine the Kansas men's basketball program, the numbers are just as alarming. "Between 2004 and 2012, 43 players who'd indicated a major in media guides have passed through the KU men's program. Of those, 61% have majored in communications, African and African-American studies, or American studies" (Hittle, 2012, para. 7).

These are just a few high profile examples of what clustering looks like and another reason why prospective African American student-athletes must do their research and ask questions before enrolling at any Division I institution.

10. Don't promote and help perpetuate tokenism. While I'm all for head coaches hiring who they want and most importantly selecting the best and most qualified person for the position, this certainly is not the case in all levels of men's and women's college basketball. I find it hard to believe that in a sport where the majority of participants are African American, these similar numbers are not translating into head and assistant coaching opportunities. I do understand why and do not agree with it, which I will get to in a moment.

Tokenism is most frequently seen on men's and women's Division I basketball staffs and to some extend many Division I football staffs. By tokenism I mean a roster comprised primarily of African American student-athletes, but there is usually one African American assistant coach or administrative staffer on a coaching staff led by a White head coach. This should be another red flag for any prospective African American student-athlete as they go through the recruiting process.

There are certainly many examples of White head coaches whose staff's do not resemble the model I described above and have consistently developed African Americans who have served as assistants under them. These White coaches have provided playing opportunities for African American student-athletes, recruiting and retaining students who are academically qualified and prepared for college, and graduating most of their African American student-athletes. Wouldn't it be reasonable to assume that if over 55% percent of Division I men's basketball players are African American, then a large number of these students could be successful head coaches at the Division I level as well or any other college level for that matter?

I understand that there are many variables to be considered when looking at the opportunity to coach a Division I basketball team. Who is actually making the hiring decision (AD, search committee, president, others)? Is the search a real search or has a candidate already been selected behind closed doors? Is the access to the opportunity really open to all qualified candidates regardless of race, and where has the opportunity been posted if at all? Are boosters influencing the decision? These are just a few ways that bright and talented African American coaching candidates can be denied access to the opportunity to become a head coach at the Division I level. As a former college basketball coach and an AD, I can personally attest that African Americans must be more qualified and work twice as hard to advance his or her career and obtain head coaching positions.

The biggest barrier, as evidenced in a 2004 study, may be many of the current White Division I head men's basketball coaches. George B. Cunningham, and Michael Sagas published *Access Discrimination in Intercollegiate Athletics* in 2004. Data from 191 Division I men's basketball programs (60% of all programs) showed that "White head coaches are more likely than Black head coaches to have White assistant coaches on staff and vice versa" (p. 148). Results of the study further indicated that the proportion of Black assistant coaches (33%) is significantly less than the proportion of potential Black coaches (48%) (Cunningham & Sagas, 2004). I would encourage you to read the entire study for additional insight into the hiring practices in Division I men's basketball.

There are several studies which have shown that while the numbers of African American student-athletes competing in Division I football, basketball, and women's basketball are increasing, the numbers of African American head coaches in these sports has remained stagnant or decreased in many years (Mirabito, 2012). On the one hand, you

ENZLEY MITCHELL IV, PH.D.

have declining racial diversity in Division I men's basketball coaching and continued exploitation of the African American student-athletes that comprise the majority of Division I rosters. The decline in the numbers of African American head men's and women's Division I basketball coaches should be a factor as prospective African American student-athletes think about where they will attend college.

A 2017 article on Athletic Business.com quoting the *Minneapolis Star Tribune*, stated, "The story of declining racial diversity on college basketball sidelines is shared coast to coast. Diversity peaked just over a decade ago, with a third of major-conference teams (23 of 70) coached by a minority in 2005. That number has fallen steadily and hit 17% (13 of 75 teams) this season, the lowest since 1995, according to a *Star Tribune* analysis of hiring in the six major basketball conferences" (Fuller, 2017, para. 3).

The point I want to make to any African American prospective student-athlete as they consider higher education institutions is to evaluate programs and coaching staffs. African American student-athletes have an obligation to not be an indirect cause of their own exploitation. Any African American student-athlete who is not aware of and who doesn't look more in depth into the makeup of their potential future coaching staff when viewed collectively is not only contributing to exploitation of African American student-athletes, but also is contributing to a decline in African American head and assistant coaches.

11. Be aware of Division I institutions where the majority of African American students by proportion are represented on the rosters of the football and basketball teams. Using the University of North Carolina at Chapel Hill (UNC) as an example, in 2012-2013, African Americans comprised 69.9% of the football and men's basketball rosters while African American males were only 3.5% of the general student population (Shuck, 2014). This number is not necessarily unique to UNC and is typical at most Power Five institutions. Why is this something that prospective African American student-athletes and their families should be aware of? In the case of UNC, it was well documented that the university benefited from the talents of African American student-athletes in football and basketball while failing to educate many of these students and not preparing them for a future in the real world. The prospective African American student-athlete and current student-athlete cannot continue to subsidize the present system and prop it up by continuing to provide labor while many receive little if any return for the investment of their time.

The many I am referring to are those student-athletes who fail to graduate and not have an opportunity to earn a living professionally after college. There is additional reason to pause during the recruiting process if the prospective African American student-athlete is borderline academically.

It is common for Division I coaches in all sports to recruit some students who may be underprepared or deficient academically due to the intense pressure to win (Mitchell, 2017). This now creates a scenario where the exploitation is compounded. Not only will an African American student in football or basketball who is underprepared academically for college not be set up for academic success and graduation, they will also still be helping generate revenue well in excess of the value of the athletic aid they receive. The risk is now twofold. This student will not receive anything beyond the value of his or her athletics scholarship. Data shows that this student has the greatest probability of not earning a degree (Jackson, 2017).

If part of the NCAA's mission is to help student-athletes receive an education that will prepare them for life after sports, why is the NCAA sitting silent? Many Power Five institutions continue to engage in academic fraud, offer no plan for any type of revenue distribution, and maintain discriminatory and unfair hiring practices. Again, if the prospective and current African American student-athletes are indirectly complicit to their own exploitation and Power Five institutions continue their current behavior, the system will not change.

12. Campus climate: Pay attention to social media and understand the social, cultural, and racial climate of any institution that is being considered and the city or region where the institution is

located. Based on the racial climate today, African American student-athletes may not be as welcome as they are let to believe during their athletics recruitment. That being said, there are some prestigious and well-known institutions that African American students just simply should not consider attending.

I think when you have a governor, university president, AD or other high ranking official that is willing to publicly criticize an African American student-athlete for expressing freedom of speech in response to current social injustices, it is a warning sign that this could be symptomatic of the institution and the region. There have been some recent instances where a high ranking official has made critical public comments toward African American students who have taken a stand based on some of the current social and racial injustices. These high-ranking officials have asserted that these and other students have no right to express themselves simply because they attend a particular institution. In nearly all recent incidents, these have been large public state institutions.

In 2016, Nebraska Governor Pete Ricketts publically criticized an African American student named Michael Rose-Ivey. Rose-Ivey played football for the University of Nebraska and took a knee before the team's game against Northwestern as a sign of protest against injustice and brutality ("Nebraska governor agrees," 2016). Governor Ricketts called the act "disgraceful and disrespectful." Two regents even criticized Rose-Ivey.

There have been additional examples of more brazen and blatant racism, which cannot be ignored by any African American student-athlete or student of color. In 2015 at the University of Oklahoma, a video surfaced showing a fraternity singing a racist song that sparked outrage and protests on campus. The 9-minute video showed members of the Sigma Alpha Epsilon fraternity chanting the N-word and exuberantly singing a racist song with references to lynching (LA Times, 2015). While the University of Oklahoma took swift action denouncing the actions of the fraternity, incidents like these are becoming more common, especially at PWIs that happen to be Power Five member institutions. For prospective African American student-athletes, the real question to ask is if continuing to attend these institutions is the best option when there are more welcoming environments.

I agree that there is a fine line here in representing your institution and First Amendment rights, but African American student-athletes continue to attend these institutions and compete for them athletically. Comments from people like Governor Ricketts basically amount to telling African American student-athletes to "shut up and play, your only value to us is on the field or on the court." The video of some members of the University of Oklahoma chapter of the Sigma Alpha Epsilon fraternity are certainly a sign of the racial feelings that lie just under the surface on the campuses of many PWIs and Power Five institutions.

Recent incidents also caught on video show how some students really feel about African Americans and other students of color. I cannot emphasize enough here how important it is to pay attention to reports of racial incidents, intimidation, and discrimination at an institution you are considering attending.

While many institutions like to publicize these incidents as being not symbolic of the entire student body, faculty, or staff, today's climate makes it easier for people to express their opinion of you and tell (or show) you how they really feel about you with no filter. Where there is smoke, there is fire.

CHAPTER 5

The Proposals
(It's Time for a Payday)

PROPOSAL 1: Net Athletics Revenue Payment (NARP). In an ideal world, my proposal would pay all NCAA Division I student-athletes across the board a stipend over and above their athletics aid and the cost of attendance. Students playing sports such as lacrosse, ice hockey, golf, tennis, and track & field would receive a stipend just as the students in the revenue sports would. But first, if you have read the previous four chapters of this book, then you will understand why the proposal would not be consistent with anything I have written. Second, it still contributes to the exploitation of a small overall demographic of student-athletes. Third, it would destroy the funding formula I am about to propose.

I keep reading and hearing about an absurd amount in the neighborhood of $5,000 that has been mentioned by the NCAA as the high end of any stipend that would be paid to student-athletes (Dodd, 2014). Some institutions could easily afford this, others would not, especially knowing that this amount would have to be paid to all student-athletes at the institution regardless of their sport and regardless of whether their sport generated a dime or operated at a loss.

As I explored how to develop a fair funding model that directly addresses the exploitation of African American student-athletes in revenue sports, many other issues that are central to the topic (race, fairness, gender equity/Title IX, amateurism, taxation, liability, and are student-athletes to be classified as employees) needs to be mentioned. At the same time as I looked deeper into how to treat African American student-athletes in the revenue sport more fairly, I find that some hard choices will need to be made if any student-athletes were going to receive money above and beyond their athletics aid.

There could be a reduction in men's sports at many institutions. Recruiting the best student-athletes in any sport would immediately become immensely more intense and competitive. The gap even in the Power Five conferences between the haves and have not's would widen. The case could be made to open dialogue with the NFL and NBA to loosen draft eligibility rules that are more in line with those in MLB and the NHL. So many things to consider.

Let us just jump right in and start by classifying all student-athletes as employees just like any other student worker, staff, faculty, or administrator at an institution. If it is determined that an amount—say $5,000—will be paid as a minimum to all student-athletes, then that should be counted as income. Students in revenue sports starting with football, men's basketball, women's basketball, and in some cases men's ice hockey and baseball, would still be able to benefit from my proposed funding model minus the annual stipend that all student-athletes would be receiving. I will provide more detail and the actual calculation for the model later in this chapter.

Now, let us allow these students to create a union or protective body as I briefly mentioned in Chapter 1. This provides the student-athletes with additional protections they are not receiving from the NCAA and their institution. Let us also begin by only implementing these changes at Power Five institutions before rolling this out across all Division I institutions. Many Power Five members will be able to pay some of the additional expenses that will come with this change such as a worker's compensation fund, federal, state, and local taxes that may be assessed, and additional institutional and national office staff needed to oversee the new system, just to name a few. Let us require as part of this new model that all student-athletes sign an addendum to any Letter of Intent or financial aid agreement that limits the liability of the institution and any fellow student-athlete in case of injury or any lawsuit.

As part of the unionization or protection process, I propose a part of the dues be set aside to fund an account to protect student-athletes and eliminate their personal exposure to any claims that may arise from a lawsuit by another student. For example, if a football player gets a penalty for unsportsmanlike conduct that results in an injury to an opponent, the opposing player would waive his right to sue and liability would be limited to a contracted amount agreed upon in the union membership contract. All income earned by institutions and students would need to be taxable unless the IRS was willing to create some specific legislation for Division I intercollegiate athletics and the potentially unionized student-athletes.

The NARP uses a formula to collect a modest portion of revenue that student-athletes help earn and is saved in an escrow account. The NARP requires no additional revenue to be generated: it simply takes a small portion of proceeds from bowl games, tournament appearances, sponsorships, apparel, shoe contracts, guarantees, TV revenue, and any other ways that revenue is generated based on the efforts of student-athletes.

I look at this the same way most institutions look at students in general. Without the student, there is no institution—no faculty, no staff, no athletics, nothing. Well, without the student-athletes, there are no shoe contracts, no apparel deals, no TV deals, no season ticket sales, etc. I think you understand what I am saying here.

As I was thinking about a fair compensation model for the students who help generate so much revenue for their institutions, I considered several things. I asked myself how could I create a model that rewards students for their hard work not only in a sport, but also outside of the field of competition while balancing their academics. I needed to come up with a model that would compensate for the time these students could not work normal part-time jobs during the school year that other students could work and summer employment. I also needed to consider why the present system is so controversial in the first place and all of the things that the revenue help to support that are good. How would my model take into consideration what the non-student-athlete would say when the amount of the student-athlete's athletics aid was taken into consideration?

As I thought about these and other things that affect the entire issue about compensating students beyond cost of attendance and a small stipend, I determined that it is best to create a formula that is not dependent on generating any additional revenue. I came up with a dual component model that gives student-athletes a small portion of the revenue they help generate while adding guidelines for an escrow account to keep the funds as they accumulate.

Based on a student's academic progress, they would be allowed to keep a percentage of their NARP. The longer they stay in school and maintain progress toward their degree, the higher percentage of their escrow account that is available to them each year. A student could take a specified amount of their NARP anytime before graduation, but would be rewarded with 100% of their NARP if they completed their eligibility and graduated from one institution. Here is how it would work:

NARP Calculation: ER X SM/Roster size = NARP deposit
Sport Individual Event Revenue X *Sport Multiplier .06 football or .02 basketball)/ Roster size (based on maximum full scholarships allowed 13 basketball or 85 football*

Example #1: (Power Five U single game NCAA tournament revenue ($1,670,000 X .02)/ Roster size of 13 = NARP deposit of $2569 per student

Example #2: Power Five U Bowl game guarantee (1,800,000 X .06)/ Roster size of 85 = NARP deposit of $1,270 per student

NARP Accumulation and Payout Chart

Year one:	Students who earn at least 30 Credit hours accepted toward their degree with a cumulative GPA of 2.5 or higher = 10% payout from NARP escrow, should the student decide to leave (transfer) their institution after completing year one. For students who continue on with their institution to year two and have declared a major other than undecided, the percentage of revenue attributed to them is deposited into their NARP account. Any student who leaves their institution has 10 years from their original enrollment date to complete their degree and to earn their full NARP account balance otherwise it is forfeited to the institution.
Year two:	Students who earn at least 60 Credit hours accepted toward their degree with a cumulative GPA of 2.5 or higher = 25% payout from NARP escrow, should the student decide to leave or (transfer) from their institution after completing year two the 25% payout available would transfer to the new institution. For students who continue on with their institution to year three, the percentage of revenue attributed to them is deposited into their NARP account. Any student who leaves their institution has 10 years from their original enrollment date to complete their degree and to earn their full NARP account balance otherwise it is forfeited to the institution.
Year three:	Students who earn at least 90 Credit hours accepted toward their with a cumulative GPA of 2.5 or higher = 50% payout from NARP escrow account, should the student decide to leave or (transfer) from their institution after completing year three, the 50% payout available would transfer to their new institution. For students who continue on with their institution to year four, the percentage of revenue attributed to them is deposited into their NARP account. Any student who leaves their institution has 10 years from their original enrollment date to complete their degree and to earn their full NARP account balance otherwise it is forfeited to the institution.
Year four:	Students who graduate with a cumulative GPA of 2.5 or higher = 100% payout from NARP escrow. Students who graduate with less than a 2.5 GPA would receive a 75% payout from their NARP account. Students who complete their eligibility, but do not graduate would receive 50% of their NARP account balance. The remainder would be paid upon proof of graduation from the institution where they completed their eligibility or any other accredited degree granting institution. Any student who leaves their institution prior to completing their eligibility has 10 years from their original enrollment date to complete their degree and to receive their full NARP account balance otherwise it is forfeited to the institution.

Benefits of the NARP plan to the Student-athlete and Institution

- The NARP rewards student-athletes for taking more than the minimum number of credit hours to remain eligible each academic year.
- The NARP encourages students to maintain a GPA at or higher than what the NCAA requires for eligibility.
- NARP funds are transferable. Should a student leave for any reason, the NARP account balance follows them to their new institution. The student has 10 years to complete their degree from their initial enrollment and receive their entire NARP account balance.
- Discourages clustering to an extent and helps students remain focused on maintaining satisfactory progress toward a degree.
- Any forfeited NARP funds would go back into the institution to help fund athletics scholarships.
- Students who transfer to an institution will begin earning their NARP from the first day they are enrolled at their new institution. Funds from any previous institution will be transferred to the student's new institution. A small retention penalty could be placed here to minimize the temptation to transfer.
- NARP provides the Student –Athlete with additional incentive to compete at a high level, achieve academic success, and maintain satisfactory progress toward their degree. This prepares students for the future and helps increase graduation rates for the institution.
- NARP encourages Student-athletes to remain committed to their institution, declare a major early and helps reduce the number of transfers.

Proposal 2: Empower U. The second idea I propose is for elite African American student-athletes in football, men's basketball, and women's basketball to broaden their view of where they take their talents when making a college choice. Think for a moment: What if just 25% of elite African American student-athletes didn't attend to a Power Five institution or any Division I institution for that matter. What if a significant percentage of these students started attending HBCUs, institutions affiliated with the NAIA, Division II, or Division III? Keep in mind that before integration of many of our colleges and universities with African American students, the NAIA and HBCUs produced the majority of elite student-athletes who went on to compete in professional football and basketball.

As integration of colleges and universities became more widespread in the late 1960s and early 1970s, these flagship institutions began accepting African American students, and they were integrated into sports teams. Participation levels of elite African American student-athletes at HBCUs and NAIA institutions dropped significantly. What if some of these students attended NAIA institutions as well as NCAA Division II and Division III institutions? Aside from the NCAA Division I HBCUs, considering these options outside of NCAA Division I remove most if not all of the revenue generation aspect and the entire exploitative nature of college sports. These students could now be competing in almost the purest form of what being a student-athlete is all about.

I propose this for the elite student-athletes only because the assumption should be that if you are talented enough to play professionally in football or basketball, you would have that God-given talent whether you attend a Division I institution, or an NAIA, or similar institution. I know there will be some who argue that the best preparation for the NFL, NBA, and WNBA occurs at the top of Division I, but there are numerous examples of exceptions African American students who have competed outside of Division I and made it to the NFL, NBA, or WNBA.

Today, fewer players are drafted into the NBA from NCAA Division II, Division III, or the NAIA due to many elite students choosing an institution based on its level and not whether it is a fit for them. Listed below is just a very small compilation of some of these students. This list certainly does not come close to addressing and listing many of the NFL and NBA Hall of Famers who competed as student-athletes in the NAIA in the 1960s and 1970s before integration. This changed the landscape of college football and basketball forever. Some of these success stories include:

Jerry Rice	Miss. Valley St. (DI HBCU)	NFL
Kyle O'Quinn	Norfolk St. (DI HBCU)	NBA
Terrance Cobb	Cumberlands (NAIA)	NFL
Andre Holmes	Hillsdale (DII)	NFL
Josephine Qwino	Union U. (NAIA)	WNBA
Cecil Shorts III	Mount Union (DIII)	NFL
William Hayes	Winston-Salem (DII HBCU)	NFL
Jahri Evans	Bloomsburg (DII)	NFL
Pierre Garson	Mount Union (DIII)	NFL
Ethan Westbrooks	W. Texas A & M (DII)	NFL
Jocquel Skinner	Bethel U. (NAIA)	NFL
Mariam Sy	Oklahoma City (NAIA)	WNBA
Donateea Dye	Heidelberg (DIII)	NFL
Robert Covington	Tennessee St. (DI HBCU)	NBA
Damon Harrison	William Penn (DII)	NFL
Terron Armstead	UAPB (DI HBCU)	NFL
Marquette King	Fort Valley (DII HBCU)	NFL
Grover Stewart	Albany State (DII HBCU)	NFL
Andrea Gardner	Howard U. (DI HBCU)	WNBA
Denzell Good	Mars Hill (DII)	NFL
Robert Mathis	Alabama A & M (DI HBCU)	NFL
Devean George	Augsburg U. (DIII)	NFL
Jerrell Freeman	Mary Hardin Baylor (DIII)	NFL
Deantre Harlan	Bacone College (NAIA)	NFL
Chad Williams	Grambling (DI HBCU)	NFL
Jessamen Dunker	Tennessee St. (DI HBCU)	NFL
Lenard Tillery	Southern U. (DI HBCU)	NFL

ENZLEY MITCHELL IV, PH.D.

CHAPTER 6

Final thoughts

IN THE INTRODUCTION to this book, I expressed my disappointment about many things related to the exploitation of student-athletes and more specifically African American student-athletes. I have researched the complexity of the changes needed at the Division I level and have listened to some leaders in college athletics make excuses about why change will occur slowly, if at all. Implementing tougher academic standards, increasing athletic aid, or offering stipends appear well intentioned on the surface, but do not go nearly far enough to elicit real change.

In a 2012 issue of *Inside Higher Ed*, Lederman quotes Mark Emmert of the NCAA from an interview:

> There is an enormous amount of uninformed, emotion-driven debate and conversation going on right now. It is clearly the case that we are in one of what has been an episodic sequence in the history of intercollegiate athletics. You have problems, and then you get a moment of change, an inflection point of ability to get things done that are very, very important. That's what we're doing. (Lederman, 2012, para. 8)

Mr. Emmert, it is just not in your own best interest or that of the NCAA to make any changes to the present system. The same goes for many of the Power Five institutions, their presidents, ADs and most football and basketball coaches at these institutions. It truly may take an act of congress to make things right, or something much simpler, and less complex. I disagree with your statement. Those at the center of this issue and the ones who provide the foundation for the entire system, the student-athletes, are much more informed than you give them credit for, and they are certainly not as emotional as you think.

My goal is to further provide prospective African American student-athletes and current African American student-athletes information and alternatives to empower themselves. My goal is also to make a proposal that works within the present system that promotes fair distribution of revenue, academic success, and ultimately helps African American student-athletes achieve their career goals after graduating. Whether that is a pro career in their sport or a career in the profession of their choosing.

The solution may be as simple as the right student-athlete saying, "No more!" It will start with one student refusing to attend a particular institution. It will then move to a team following through on boycotting an athletics competition and inspiring others to do the same. It will take many students not just African American students to make a sacrifice and being willing to take a different route.

I challenge all student-athletes to make the change that needs to happen. I challenge current African American student-athletes in the revenue sports to not wait another season and take a stand together to make change happen now! Change will be painful. These changes may cause a reduction in men's sports. Institutions will need to consider if some sports should be only offered as club sports. This may mean reducing the number of varsity sports offered at some institutions. This could mean dropping the use of the term *amateur* in intercollegiate athletics. At some point, this ill certainly mean at some point that some students will be paid and that the tax exemption that the NCAA, colleges, and universities have enjoyed may go away.

It will not take a monumental act to allow African American student-athletes to begin to eliminate the exploitation some of them face. Change will occur quickest with their White peers standing shoulder to should with them. These students could go it alone, but why? Win as a team, lose as team, so why stand-alone?

REFERENCES

Bauer-Wolf, J. (2018, March 12). Distorting the record on Black male athletes: New report calls out NCAA for saying that black athletes graduate at higher rates than other black students, when that's not true at the top conferences. *Inside Higher ED*. Retrieved from https://www.insidehighered.com/news/2018/03/12/graduation-rates-black-athletes-lower-most-students-study-shows

Berkowitz, S. (2013, July 10). Emmert made $1.7 million, according to NCAA tax return. *USA Today*. Retrieved from https://www.usatoday.com/story/sports/college/2013/07/10/ncaa-mark-emmert-salary-million-tax-return/2505667/

Brown, G. T. (2014). *Mind, body, and sport understanding and supporting student-athlete mental wellness*. Retrieved from https://www.naspa.org/images/uploads/events/Mind_Body_and_Sport.pdf

Chung, D. J. (2013). *The dynamic advertising effect of college athletics* (Position paper). Harvard Business School. Retrieved from http://www.hbs.edu/faculty/Publication%20Files/13-067_99c551d6-c484-4245-9e49-964d2283cd98.pdf

Cunningham, G. B., & Sagas, M. (2005, May). Access discrimination in intercollegiate athletics. *Journal of Sport and Social Issues, 29*(2), 148-163.

Dodd, D. (2014, January 15). Paying athletes figures to be key issue at annual NCAA convention. *CBS Sports*. Retrieved from https://www.cbssports.com/college-football/news/paying-athletes-figures-to-be-key-issue-at-annual-ncaa-convention/

Duara, N., & Hennessy-Fiske, M. (2015, March 14). Furor over Oklahoma fraternity's racist song may lead to lasting changes. *Los Angeles Times*. Retrieved from http://www.latimes.com/nation/nationnow/la-na-ff-sae-oklahoma-20150314-story.html

Fuller, M. (2017, March). *Where have the Black college coaches gone?* Retrieved from https://www.athleticbusiness.com/college/where-have-the-black-college-basketball-coaches-gone.html

Harper, S. R. (2018, March 12). Black male student-athletes and racial inequities in NCAA division I college sports. *Inside Higher ED*. Retrieved from https://www.insidehighered.com/news/2018/03/12/graduation-rates-black-athletes-lower-most-students-study-shows

Hawkins, B. (2010). *The new plantation: Black athletes, college sports, and predominantly White NCAA institutions*. New York, NY: Palgrave McMillan.

Harper, S. R., Williams, C. D., & Blackman, H. W. (2013). *Black male student-athletes and racial inequities in NCAA division I college sports*. Retrieved from https://equity.gse.upenn.edu/sports2016

Hittle, S. (2012, March 6). Archive for Friday, June 15, 2012: Athletes' tendencies to "cluster" in certain academic fields problematic, some say. *Lawrence Journal-World*. Retrieved from http://www2.ljworld.com/news/2012/jun/15/athletes-tendencies-cluster-certain-academic-field/

Jackson, D. Z. (2017, May 31). *NCAA ban of 15 HBCU teams from postseason play is polite racism if regulators looked honestly at the academic progress of black athletes, major Division I programs would be censured too*. Retrieved from https://theundefeated.com/features/ncaa-ban-15-hbcu-teams-postseason-play-is-polite-racism/

Joiner, L. L. (2016, June 19). Off the court: Are colleges preparing gifted athletes for life after sports? *NBC News*. Retrieved from https://www.nbcnews.com/news/nbcblk/court-are-colleges-preparing-gifted-athletes-life-after-sports-n595291

Lapchick, R. E. (2017). 2017 *College sports racial & gender report card*. The Institute for Diversity and Ethics in Sports. Retrieved from http://nebula.wsimg.com/5665825afd75728dc0c45b52ae6c412d?AccessKeyId=DAC3A56D8FB782449D2A&disposition=0&alloworigin=1

Lederman, D. (2012, January 10). College sports reform: Now? Never? *Inside Higher ED*. Retrieved from https://www.insidehighered.com/news/2012/01/10/calls-major-reform-college-sports-unlikely-produce-meaningful-change

Kopkin, N. (2014). You're fired!: The impact of race on the firing of Black head coaches in major college football. *The Review of Black Political Economy, 41*(4), 373–392.

Mitchell IV, E. (2017). *The Significance of family, environment, and college preparation: A study of factors influencing graduation and persistence rates of African American males playing division I basketball* (Doctoral dissertation). Ann Arbor, MI: ProQuest LLC.

Mirabito, T. (2012, November 19). Black coaches trying to make it in a White-dominated industry: College football and the racial divide. *The Sport Journal.* Retrieved from http://thesportjournal. org/article/black-coaches-trying-to-make-it-in-a-white-dominated-industry-college-football-and-the-racial-divide/

NAIA. (n.d.). *About the NAIA.* Retrieved from http://www.naia.org/ViewArticle.dbml?DB_OEM_ID=27900&ATCLID=211686810

NCAA. (n.d.).*Where does the money go?* Retrieved from http://www. ncaa.org/about/where-does-money-go

Nebraska governor agrees to meet with Huskers' anthem protester. (2016, March 9). *USA Today.* Retrieved from https://www.usatoday. com/story/sports/ncaaf/2016/09/27/nebraska-anthem-protesters-draw-ire-of-2-regents-governor/91192088/

New, J. (2016, July 8). An "epidemic" of academic fraud. *Inside Higher ED.* Retrieved from https://www.insidehighered.com/news/2016/07/08/more-dozen-athletic-programs-have-committed-academic-fraud-last-decade-more-likely

Nichols, A., & Evans Bell, D. (2017). A look at Black student success identifying top- and bottom-performing institutions. *The Education Trust.* Retrieved from https://edtrust.org/resource/black-student-success/

Schroeder, G. (2017, June 28). NCAA proposal would stop schools, coaches from holding transfers hostage. *USA Today.* Retrieved from https://www.usatoday.com/story/sports/college/2017/06/28/ncaa-proposal-ease-path-for-transfers/437306001/

Shuck, J. R. (2014, December). Academic racism in play in regards to athletes. *Diverse: Issues in Higher Education.* Retrieved from http://diverseeducation.com/article/68277/

Silverman, R. (2015, November 11). What if NCAA athletes boycotted for wages? Retrieved from https://www.thedailybeast.com/what-if-ncaa-athletes-boycott-for-wages

Trahan, K. (2014, August). How The NCAA's Marxist philosophy is hurting its athletes. *Forbes/SportsMoney*. Retrieved from https://www.forbes.com/sites/kevintrahan/2014/08/18/how-the-ncaa-hurts-the-players-it-claims-to-protect/#650dbf2018e5

Racist graffiti found written in chalk on sidewalks at the university of Oregon. (2018, January). *The Journal of Blacks in Higher Education*. Retrieved from https://www.jbhe.com/2018/01/racist-graffiti-found-written-in-chalk-on-sidewalks-at-the-university-of-oregon/

Racists signs posted on the campus of the University of South Carolina. (2018, January). *The Journal of Blacks in Higher Education*. Retrieved from https://www.jbhe.com/2018/01/racists-signs-posted-on-the-campus-of-the-university-of-south-carolina/

University of Alabama expels White woman after she posted racist videos. (2018, January). *The Journal of Blacks in Higher Education*. Retrieved from https://www.jbhe.com/2018/01/university-of-alabama-expels-white-woman-after-she-posted-racist-videos/

Wallsten, K., Nteta, T. M., McCarthy, L. A., & Tarsi, M. R. (2017). Prejudice or principled conservatism? Racial resentment and White opinion toward paying college athletes. *Political Research Quarterly, 70*(1), 209–222.

Whaley, N. (2013, July 22). *I'm tired of my Blackness being a problem*. Retrieved from http://heartsconverse.com/2013/07/22/im-tired-of-my-blackness-being-a-problem/

Wilson, G., Sakura-Lemessy, I., & West, J. P. (1999). Reaching the top: Racial differences in mobility paths to upper-tier occupations. *Work and Occupations, 26*(2), 165-186.